MAYBE YOU SHOULD WRITE A BOOK

MAYBE YOU SHOULD WRITE A BOOK

RALPH DAIGH

Prentice-Hall, Inc., Englewood Cliffs, New Jersey

Maybe You Should Write a Book, by Ralph Daigh
Copyright © 1977 by Ralph Daigh

Printed in the United States of America
Prentice-Hall International, Inc., London
Prentice-Hall of Australia, Pty. Ltd., Sydney
Prentice-Hall of Canada, Ltd., Toronto
Prentice-Hall of India Private Ltd., New Delhi
Prentice-Hall of Japan, Inc., Tokyo
Prentice-Hall of Southeast Asia Pte. Ltd., Singapore
Whitehall Books Limited, Wellington, New Zealand
10 9

Library of Congress Cataloging in Publication Data

Daigh, Ralph.
    Maybe you should write a book.
    1. Authorship.   I. Title.
PN145.D27   808'.025   76-54952
ISBN 0-13-566380-6
ISBN-0-13-566372-5 pbk.

CONTENTS

Contents

MAYBE YOU SHOULD WRITE A BOOK

MAYBE YOU SHOULD WRITE A BOOK

I want to give you every possible help and encouragement to write a book if that has been your dream.

Many of those who have said to themselves or friends, "Someday I am going to write a book," are capable, and some actually will write a book and have it published. Some version of that phrase, "I'm going to write a book," has preceded the actual writing of a book by every author.

My nagging conviction and observation is that many, many persons have avoided becoming successful authors because they simply did not make the effort to write that book. Instead they permitted other interests, accomplishments, and involvements to sidetrack and suppress their urge to write.

Of course not everyone who has dreamed that dream could write a publishable book and I do not want to give false hope to those unqualified.

Yet the requirements for successful authorship are, judging by those who have made a success of writing, so shadowy, so minimal, so lacking in precise definition that to point a finger at anyone willing to try and say: "You can't write a book!" would be stupidly dictatorial.

In the final decision of whether to write a book, you will have to judge your own qualifications and ambition, but this book will help you make the judgment.

If you decide you *will* write a book, I have presented considerable information, suggestions, and encouragement for you. In addition more than twenty very successful authors' experiences in learning to write, and as writers, make up a considerable part of this book.

I have a stubborn, unshakable conviction that there are thousands of individuals with the latent ability (and whatever else it takes) to write successful books; yet they have not done so.

After many years as an editor, editorial director, and publisher of magazines and books, I am convinced that the single biggest reason more people have not written books is that they have not found, or been given, encouragement to make the attempt.

Indeed, anyone daring to announce his intent to become an author is more likely to evoke discouraging snickers of doubt than words of encouragement.

Even the publishing industry has done far more to discourage aspiring writers than to help and encourage them.

But not me! My entire purpose here is to encourage qualified persons to write books—not one book, but two, three, four and more; to become, if that is your goal, a full-fledged professional author.

Just so you will know something of the directions we are taking, I'll give you a hint of what to expect.

You are going to get several bases for comparison so you may measure your natural abilities and background preparation for authorship against those of others who have managed to make successful careers as writers.

Also, you are going to get a tiny look at what goes on behind the scenes in publishing, because so many would-be authors have demonstrated a curiosity about the business. Many, before actually attempting to write, have gone so far as to have deliberately—and mistakenly—secured employment as editors. Besides, anyone weighing the possibility of a writing career is entitled to have some knowledge of the publishing business.

I confess still another reason: a desire to rip a hole in the cocoon of mystique which publishing has woven around itself. Once you see through this hole, you will observe that ghosts of the gods and saints of literature do not swoop and glide over the heads of persons on the publishing premises like some animated halo. The editors and other employees do not tiptoe and whisper as in a holy place, or genuflect to statue shrines of Chaucer, Melville, James, and Shakespeare. No indeed!

Instead these able people drink coffee from paper cups and work long hours, intelligently (for the most part) and hard. The music you hear is not that of the celestial spheres but the hum of modern computers.

There are, too, the heady breathtaking emotions that attend high-stake poker as publishers compete in the gamble to place books in the best-seller category, where rewards are astronomical for author and publisher.

I want you to know publishing for what it is—a business, a booming business. It is also a rather rough, tough, highly competitive business—very lacking in lace cuffs, lorgnettes, and other attributes of phony culture. It is, of course, all the more interesting and satisfying for those reasons.

The first seldom-admitted or even realized fact of publishing I want to present for your selfish encouragement and eye-opening contemplation is this:

There are very, very few really good books published.

This because there is, and always has been, an absolute dearth of, lack of, paucity of superior authors and superior manuscripts.

Proof of this appalling scarcity of authors and manuscripts is ever naked and shivering before us—the hundreds, even thousands, of books that get published that are patently, obviously bad. Many of these are books that neither reader nor reviewer can speak well of, but which are published because they are the best editors can find.

And some of these "bad" books, books that are crudely done or offensively frank, have, surprisingly, been known to become best-sellers—usually because they possessed a quality or honesty that overcame their deficiencies of style or professional expertise.

But don't get the idea that you can quickly and easily write and sell a second-rate inferior novel or book. You can take some solace from the fact that the competition is not any stronger than it is, but if you are successful in writing and securing publication of a book, you will only do so as a result of unstinting application of your abilities and hard work that may surpass in difficulty any task you have ever attempted.

And the pure joy and satisfaction you experience as a result of finishing the task of writing a book may well be the greatest joy and satisfaction of your life.

Again, don't assume the writing of a book to be easy. If you are not prepared to work as hard at writing as you are intelligently capable of doing, and rewriting until you believe you have done your best, don't attempt to write books.

Further proof of the woesome lack of good manuscripts lies in the enormous prices now being paid authors for the competitively superior books—novels or nonfiction.

It may be that you are not motivated to write by the lure of gold, that your ambition is to add to literature rather than to your bank balance. That's okay, too, but the fact is that even books of a "literary" type are literally earning fortunes for their authors; specifically, works of Saul Bellow, John Updike, John Barth, Joyce Carol Oates, and others.

Books that can combine literary value and popular appeal literally sell for what might be called "a hijacker's dream."

Such a book is *Centennial* by James A. Michener, for which Fawcett guaranteed a million dollars for the right to reprint the book in paperback on a relatively short-term license. In addition, the deserving author will get very large earnings from other sources, including book clubs, hardcover editions, foreign language rights, motion picture rights, and so forth.

That information I regard as an undisguised gold-colored carrot with which I hope to arouse an envious twitching of your nose. It is only one instance in which vast sums have been paid for books. I intend to tell you about others, too. Not just to emphasize the shortage of competitive book manuscripts, but as proof that the public is starving for good books, that book publishing—and book writing—is big business and is here to stay.

If that were not so, Fawcett would not pay a million dollars for reprint rights to *Centennial*. It is because of the hunger for good books by millions of readers that Fawcett can sell millions of copies of *Centennial* in paperback; thus recover the million dollar investment and, hopefully, make a profit.

Of further interest to you is the fact that authors capable, or thought to be capable, of writing best-sellers are literally being "stolen" by some publishers, one from the other, with increasing frequency and wanton boldness. This is, of course, both a moral reflection on the thieves and a competitive reflection of the manuscript shortage.

Yes, it is a seller's market, and the seller is the proven author with a manuscript in his briefcase.

In spite of that circumstance here is another fact that may surprise you and many persons in book publishing:

Despite intense competition among publishers for proven best-selling authors and high prices paid for manuscripts deemed to be potential best-sellers, the book publishing industry has done more to *discourage* would-be authors than to help them.

Proof of this longtime policy of lack of encouragement lies, tragically, in the fact that a telephone-conducted poll revealed almost a third of the nation's book publishers still return unsolicited manuscripts unread.

But the percentage of those who do read the "slush" is increasing. Only a short year ago an estimated one half of all publishers returned such manuscripts unread.

This longtime lack of encouragement is saddening because many of you who desire to write are as adequately prepared for authorship as those who have persevered, fought, and even "lucked" their way to writing fame; and there is nothing wrong with lucking your way if you can do it.

What is the basic preparation for authorship?

Nothing but the common mechanics of writing: spelling, grammar, syntax, which most of you have learned in school.

Yet many authors have had a minimum of schooling. Louis L'Amour left school at fifteen; Harold Robbins dropped out even earlier. These men, however, learned grammar and spelling elsewhere. Some successful writers, surprisingly, do not know the common rules of grammar and depend on copy editors and secretaries to correct spelling and bad grammar in their manuscripts. This kind of ignorance must not be reflected in a submitted manuscript—unless it is your ambition to become a collector of rejection slips.

In other words, the accepted mechanics of writing, spelling, grammar, and so forth represents one of two bags of tools employed by writers.

The other bag of tools is possessed by everyone, but only by actually writing will you learn if these tools are sharp enough, unique enough, and appreciated enough so that you can shape a successful career as an author, particularly an author of fiction. This second bag is the one that contains everything that has shaped and molded you into the person you are. This is indeed a complex assortment and includes every memory (conscious and unconscious) of everything you have experienced or dreamed, every prejudice, and everything inherited and acquired that has made you, you. These are your own exclusive tools, unduplicated elsewhere, and these are the tools with which you will shape your own unique identity as a writer.

If your ambition is to become a novelist, the single most important prerequisite is having read and enjoyed many novels. Your reading should have started at an early age and should have been widely varied and unflagging.

Perhaps your ambition is not to write novels, but books of a factual nature—anything from textbooks to best-sellers about personal experiences. If nonfiction writing is your goal, it would be helpful if your background and training included experiences that involve communicating information through the written or spoken word. Experience as a newspaper reporter, a clergyman, a teacher, or an attorney, or the ability to write letters of great human interest or to exhibit skill and persuasion in talking or writing are all encouraging evidences of your possible writing skills.

Still another background qualification that may lead you to successful nonfiction authorship is expertise and specialized knowledge in any subject from anthropology or astrology to xylophones, yoga, or Zen. Our reading public has demonstrated a great interest in acquiring knowledge on subjects about which they are uninformed, and they appreciate learning it from experts. Particularly, there is a market for the specialized writer who can translate the highly technical and obscure subjects into easily understood everyday language.

Such specialized books have included such mundane, unlikely subjects as American business methods or contemporary history.

In the first category, American business, is included an easy-to-read book that led the best-seller lists for many months, *Up the Organization*, by Robert Townsend. This was the author's first book. Fawcett paid a guaranteed advance against royalties of $275,000 for paperback reprint rights.

In the second category, contemporary history, is the famous *The Rise and Fall of the Third Reich* by veteran journalist William L. Shirer, for which Fawcett paid, in 1961, a then record-breaking $400,000, against royalties earned. Prices have gone up since then.

Nonfiction book categories are limitless—from best-sellers about a teacher's classroom experiences to cookbooks written by housewives, including a cookbook jape by puckish Peg Bracken called *The I Hate to Cook Book*, whose sales exceed a million copies.

We might include too a charming little best-seller called *That Quail, Robert*, a book written by a housewife concerning a small wild bird that adopted a New England family. Or, in a wide swing of factual subject matter, the enormous best-seller, *The Joy of Sex*, appetizingly edited and so intimately illustrated that author and publisher have made millions of dollars from sales of a book on perhaps the oldest of popular subjects.

So far you have seen considerable reference to money, big money, paid to writers for their books. I want to point out that money is useful, is satisfying to possess in quantity, and its accumulation is very supportive of an author's ego.

In putting this emphasis on the large sums you as an author may earn, I hope to demonstrate that the single most vital contribution, without which the commercial industry of publishing could not

6

function, is the author's manuscript. It is worth every dollar it is capable of earning.

Money makes the publishing wheels go around, whether they be the wheels on presses, the delivery trucks in the circulation department, the chauffeur-driven limousine of the publisher, the sports car for the editor, or the stable of foreign cars of the author. As an author you are entitled to your share. What you do with it—give it away, keep it, or spend it—is your decision, but don't scorn it.

Because the whole purpose of this book is to encourage those qualified to write books, I feel it is necessary to point out in some detail the large potential for earning money by writing. It may be that such rewards do not motivate you, but stay around anyway. I shall have examples of other rewards of authorship that may have more appeal for you.

This book is not concerned with teaching you to write. I am inclined to view such books as dangerous and more likely to destroy an individual's potential for writing than to nurture it. I happen to believe, too, that teachers of writing can not successfully teach writing, and those who persist in such efforts contribute more to despair, failure, and bad writing than to successful writing.

Now and then there is a teacher of writing wise enough not to teach writing, but who guides his pupils by indirection into paths of learning that will encourage his writing without telling him how to do it. This teacher is a listener, a giver of a limited amount of criticism—if he gives any at all.

Somerset Maugham is credited with summing it all up when in addressing a friend's class on English literature he was asked by a student how to write a novel.

Maugham's answer was:

"There are three rules for the writing of a novel.

"Unfortunately no one knows what they are."

Recently some forty persons each paid $110 to attend a weekend literary activity at Tarrytown, New York, under the sponsorship of *Saturday Review/World* magazine, including a seminar conducted by editors from New York publishing houses. Most of those attending seemed to be aspiring writers and they gave an audible, concerted groan when Marilyn Durham, author of *The Man Who Loved Cat Dancing*, an unusually successful first novel said: "No one can teach you writing. You have to learn it yourself."

I too am of the opinion that you must teach yourself to write novels. Certainly more successful novelists have taught themselves their craft than have learned their skills from teachers.

7

I believe those would-be authors at the seminar should have given a collective cheer, rather than a concerted groan, when Miss Durham said: "No one can teach you writing. You have to learn it yourself."

A cheer instead of a groan because it is the creative aspect of writing that makes writing so rewarding, both emotionally and financially. Quite obviously, if writing could be reduced to the level of a learned exercise such as memorizing the multiplication tables, rewards—personal or financial—would be minimal.

You, or anyone who seeks to write, should rejoice that whatever form your writing takes—whether you are a novelist or a reporter—your writing is a personal creation uniquely your own, implanted and fertilized not by pedagogy, but by your experiences, observations, sensory perceptions, and imagination.

I was once among the audience listening to Artur Rubinstein, perhaps the most admired and most famous modern piano virtuoso. With great earnestness and conviction, he said in substance: "A person cannot be taught to become a musician. It is something you are born with. Something you must do. Then you can become a musician by practice, by working with and observing other musicians, but you cannot be taught to become a musician."

It may be a far reach from being a musician to being a novelist, but both share many common distinctions, and I believe what Rubinstein says about musicians is also true about novelists. You cannot be taught to be a novelist. Practice in writing, observation of others who are novelists, and reading their works is the proper and most often-used road by those who achieve success in this field.

Much has been written about the pleasures of creativity, the surging, emotional, animalistic satisfaction that comes from giving birth to offspring or expression. It is a writer's good fate to experience this earthy pleasure with some frequency, and also his fate to experience the unhappiness that comes with failure to accomplish exactly what he desires in his written expression, or even to come acceptably close.

Maybe here is the place to warn you again that writing is hard work, and anyone not willing to approach authorship as a job requiring complete dedication and every necessary sacrifice should not aspire to the profession.

If any accomplishment by humans deserves to be called "self-acquired," it is that of writing.

This book presents to you in some detail how successful authors have met and solved problems of authorship, but it in no sense teaches you how to write, it only encourages you to find your own way.

I hope you do not find it contradictory that it is not possible to teach writing successfully, yet it is possible for one author to aid another by indirection and example. In this way your style of writing and even your thinking may be influenced by authors you have read widely and admired or disliked. This is all to the good, but you don't receive a profit from having instructions, truisms, and axioms crammed into your cranium.

If it helps you, imitate other writers' work schedules—whether from midnight to 6:00 A.M., as some are, or from 9:00 A.M. to noon, as others are.

Certainly, too, you are not compromising yourself by learning how an author approaches the actual planning of a novel. Is there an outline? Is the ending planned before all else? (Some say yes.) What research is done and how? How does the author get the first words on paper? How extensive is rewriting?

You will get answers to such questions in this book.

You will find that writers confess to experiencing the same problems, but their solutions vary. Perhaps from reading these solutions you will learn in which direction you can go most happily and profitably as a writer.

A writer is entitled to learn from any source he can find and in any manner he can devise. If he is worthy of the title "author," he cannot slavishly assume the writing identity or methods of expression of another and thus destroy himself.

Even as doctors, lawyers, and other professionals profit by associating with, and exchanging information with, their colleagues, so do writers profit by the exchange of ideas and methods.

It is my hope that you will find more useful, encouraging information of that sort in these pages than you will find in any other single source.

There will be some other incidental bits and pieces of information, possibly not directly connected with your decision to be a writer. Perhaps the insight you may gain into publishing will lead you to an editing career.

In either case I trust I shall be able to destroy completely any concept that authorship or the publishing industry has a halo of divinity hanging eerily over it, a bit of ectoplasm that indicates publishing is a world unreal and apart. There is no more mystique to writing and publishing than there is to any other kind of manufacturing, but the world of writing and publishing is populated by more imaginative, erudite, interesting, delightful people than any other industry I know.

On that score I would not deny that the industry has a definite glamour, and there is no mistaking that such glamour comes only from the authors. Long-haired publishers and witty editors have only a sort of secondhand reflected glamour. Authors are the ones in our world today who have replaced movie stars as glamour figures.

As we go along I hope to show you there is no more mystique to authorship or the publishing industry than there is to house building, banking, engineering, or any other profession where imagination and intelligent human application produce useful results. "Mystique" should be applied to acupuncture, hypnosis, or three-cushioned billiards.

WHAT QUALIFIES YOU TO BECOME A WRITER?

Do you really want to write? Have you felt a recurring urge to express yourself on paper? Did you get a warm, satisfying sense of elation while writing (and thus creating) a theme, an essay, or story in your school days? Have you written some short stories or a novel that did not sell; or started one—or several—without finishing any?

If you can answer yes to most or all of those questions, you can take some encouragement from the fact that in so doing you are meeting a writer's first requirement—you want to write.

Without that gnawing, recurring desire to write, do not attempt authorship. If you have such a desire, acknowledge that you are in a small elite group distinguished by a desire to write.

This group is smaller than you think, in case you fear the world is teeming with would-be authors.

The very fact that you want to write displays a degree of intelligent imagination on your part, a kind of imagination not shared by those who do not have a desire to be writers. Look about you on the street, or among those persons you know, and you will realize those with no desire, hope, or thought of writing vastly outnumber those with the dream.

Given the desire to write, who can say that individual will not write a novel or nonfiction book? Only that individual himself.

Once you are sure of your desire and ambition, you need only to make the sincere effort to write a book. The desire qualifies you for the effort and the lack of desire in others rules out the possibility of authorship for them.

10

There is an inclination on my part to stress the desirability of some specialized or college education as a background for authorship. A degree of any sort gives its holder confidence and, hopefully, some specialized knowledge. The obtaining of a degree reflects self-discipline and a background of information whether it's in liberal arts, education, business administration, or engineering. Whatever the field, the knowledge and interests you gain in pursuing your degree should help shape your identity as a writer and influence the subjects you choose to write about.

But, actually, such education is not a necessity, provided you have whatever it is that has made successful writers out of thousands of individuals who did not have a formal education.

Harold Robbins, mentioned earlier, has made millions from books and screen plays, such as *The Betsy* and *The Pirate*. He was abandoned at a Catholic orphanage, farmed out to a Jewish family, ran away at age fifteen, dropped out of school, and through a series of improbable adventures of his own fashioning went on to become a Hollywood scriptwriter and finally a modern commercial novelist. He's the kind of writer publishers attempt to pilfer from one another with seductive talk of "contract terms to better suit your artistry and increased royalty rate." This form of "kidnapping" is more remunerative than robbing banks, and is without a jail-term penalty for the publisher.

Mark Twain made more than a mark for himself as an author, yet he had very little schooling. Louis L'Amour, prolific and successful writer of westerns, did not finish high school; neither did Nobel-Prize-Winner-for-Literature William Faulkner. Faulkner's novels have been translated into thirty-two languages and two of them were awarded the Pulitzer Prize.

It is something of a surprise that Faulkner, whose writing has always been categorized as "literary," did not finish high school; and it wasn't because he could not afford to go to school. His father was a banker.

Faulkner was not, however, without education and as a boy displayed a marked creative ability in drawing. He read widely at an early age and wrote poetry, but he did not sell anything until he was twenty-two. At age nineteen he took some scattered courses at the University of Mississippi while clerking at his father's bank, but he never received a degree. He worked for a short period in a New York City book store then returned to Oxford, Mississippi, where he was a postmaster at the university postal station for three years. Faulkner's first published writings were poems and short stories and his most successful novels were not written until he had earned a reputation, and big money in those days, as a Hollywood script-writer. It was Faulkner's boast that he was "uneducated in every formal sense, without very literate, let alone literary, companions."

So, formal education isn't always necessary, and neither is education, per se, enough. In addition you will have to apply yourself as wholeheartedly and with the dedication someone else might apply to the study of medicine, law, or engineering. Let's hope, too, you have the kind of luck that always seems to follow people like Harold Robbins—those guys who won't give up.

If you are making this "decision for authorship" in your youth, possibly as an alternate to law, medicine, or the family business, it is only logical that you look carefully over the potential of this profession financially and from every other aspect. After all, there is nothing that says you must be a writer simply because you feel an urge to write.

I'm not going to say much about the advantages of an author's life-style other than to point out that the professional writer of ability will pay a large income tax and will pretty much go where he wants to go and do what he wants to do. Later on you will learn a great deal from the writers themselves about their life-styles; mostly, it seems, all they want to do is write.

Some authors have an active interest in sports. Many play tennis and similar sports enthusiastically and for fun. Very few play golf determinedly or regularly, for the obvious reason that golf takes too much time away from the sport they like best—writing.

Most authors read a lot and travel a lot. The stimulation of new places, new vistas, and new people seems to stir the creative juices; you will find that many authors get a new book out of each trip. When such is the case, one of the advantages is that it is possible to write off a considerable part of the trip's expenses on your income tax return. Thus, you get paid for traveling.

A few authors drink a lot, but not when they are writing. Certainly they do not drink as much as editors—those with the ready excuse for the three-martini business lunch. Also, some editors are inclined to drink excessively because they are frustrated writers; and frustration plus an expense account makes drinking easy, tempting, and inexpensive. Not being as frustrated as editors, authors sometimes invent other reasons for drinking, but generally they have an undeserved reputation as drunks. This is due, I'm sure, to the well-publicized alcoholic antics of Brendan Behan, F. Scott Fitzgerald, and a few other alcoholic "sickies." Successful authors find the heady process of creating more stimulating than booze and do not drink to excess, in my observation.

Some authors suffer a lot from adverse critical reviews of their writings, but such wounds heal quickly without the salve of drink, particularly if the book sells well.

I've known some authors that took sex pretty seriously as a sport, including one who added a fresh, and in this case "needed" touch of novelty to his honeymoon night by setting off a string of firecrackers under the nuptial bed at a precisely calculated moment. I've known some, too, who professed to approach sex with a sober air of investigative research, in the interest of their career experience. To my knowledge none of these made notes while so engaged. A surprising number of authors, particularly women authors, remain with their first mates. This may be a reflection that such women are usually very good providers in the crass and materialistic sense, and, in a few instances, have attracted a mate who is willing to sit back and observe, or even take ten percent of their wife's earnings as her agent. It may be, of course, that they are just ideal mates, intellectually and emotionally.

What I want you to do now is cast an appraising eye on some of the current economic facts concerning authorship and the publishing business as well as its future prospects, and then to decide whether publishing is an economically safe business with which to associate yourself. This is a particularly serious and important consideration for a young person weighing the possibility of authorship as a lifetime profession. But it is important, too, to anyone, young or old, who contemplates devoting time and effort to writing books.

I am going to tip my hand as to the economic opportunity of authorship by saying that parents of a marriageable daughter should no longer have fainting spells at the news that the daughter is going to marry a writer. Her married life might well be more unsatisfactory economically if she were to marry a lawyer or a doctor. And if she too is a writer, now that women enjoy their new independence by doing "creative" things, such a sharing as is represented in a writer-married-to-writer is boundless in its promise.

Do you think the situation of a husband and wife both authors impossible? Don't scorn it. As the market for manuscripts has grown, many wives of writers, or husbands of writers, as the case may be, and even sons and daughters of authors, have turned to writing successfully.

Irving Wallace's family has received the most publicity in this respect. Not only is Irving continuing to attempt to fill the world's yawning need for novels single-handedly, but his wife has written a book and seen it published as has the daughter of the family and the son. They have done well as first authors with advances in the $50,000 range. Each is writing another book.

Less widely sung but equally interesting evidence of families declaring for authorship successfully is the Yglesias family which left Manhattan's upper West Side and opened what can be described as a successful family book-writing enterprise in North Brooklin, Maine. The father, José, was forty-three when he produced his first novel, then left behind a career that included a dozen years as an executive for a large pharmaceutical company Merck Sharp & Dohme. Rafael, Mr. and Mrs. Yglesias' son, published his first novel on his sixteenth birthday, almost simultaneously with his mother's first novel, a book she started work on at age fifty-four. Included in this snug little "writery" is Mrs. Yglesias' son by a previous marriage, also a writer. This is no recent family effort. Mr. Yglesias turned full-time writer in 1969 and that is when the family moved to Maine. Since then Mrs. Yglesias has published two novels, Rafael two, and José eight. And each is deep into a new book.

Gone is the poverty-and-garret existence that was both real and traditional for the writer in times past. Instead, the professional writer, one who works hard and successfully at his trade, has tax problems, but they were somewhat alleviated recently by an IRS provision that permits authors to spread large short-period incomes, such as a movie sale, over a period of several years.

The fact is, book publishing has entered into an expansion period from which there seems no possible retreat, except, possibly, an infrequent and tiny flattening in the cyclical sale curve due to recent and dramatic increase in book prices. Everything in the business is expanding. Book reading is expanding—and that is the most important index of all. Publishers' sales are expanding. Authors' profits are expanding. Overall, the expansion is far larger than many persons in the business are aware of, or will admit.

More books are being sold. More books are being read than ever before. Readers are demonstrating a hunger for reading that makes multimillion-copy best-sellers out of books not entitled to such sales. Our best-seller lists are cluttered with patently inferior titles, books are being bought in dramatic quantities because they are the best of the available "not-too-good" lot.

It is the reading public that has caused this publishing explosion. In the ever increasing purchase of books, readers have demonstrated a voracious appetite. Publishers are running their presses, in some cases, on twenty-four-hour shifts, seven days a week (double time on Sunday) to slake this appetite. It's a losing race, because the more a reader reads, the more he wants to read, until it must be accepted that reading, particularly for entertainment, is addictive.

There are obvious reasons for this explosion. The most obvious and volatile contributor to the pyrotechnics is the low-price paperback book. The "mass" paperback book in the sense we know it today was first published in England, in a line still published called Penguin Books. The idea was imitated and imported into this country in 1939 under the imprint, Pocket Books.

Early progress of Pocket Books was slow and sales were low, as distribution facilities adjusted themselves to the new concept of twenty-five-cent books. However, sales increased steadily enough to encourage competition, and other publishers came into the paperback field with the imprints of Bantam, Dell, Avon, Signet, and, in 1950, Fawcett.

It wasn't until five years later, in 1955, that the slumberous world of publishing awoke to the fact that the loud noises, the shaking of the very industry foundations, was not caused by blasting in the subway. The grinding and churning was the noisy and violent expansion of the paperback industry; and the loud noises were accompanied by the agreeable tinkling of gold. Suddenly publishers of what some called "those flimsy little paper-covered books," began paying hardcover publishers more money for reprint licenses to authors' works than anyone had ever dreamed was possible.

The American public had gone on a reading jag. People everywhere were buying books in bunches, like grapes or bananas—not just a book once a year for someone's birthday gift.

Instead of a title selling only 1,500 to 3,000 copies in hardcover, or a once-in-a-while 10,000, the paperback editions were selling 100,000, 300,000, and even more.

These revolutionary large sales did not develop until the late 1940s and early 1950s, and sales did not really fly into the multimillion area until after 1955.

No doubt of it. The success of the cheap paperbound book is the most dramatic influence upon book publishing since the invention of printing. It is the paperback book that has made book publishing and authorship stable, profitable, and altogether desirable enterprises.

Particularly has it made authorship an enviable, much-to-be desired, highly rewarding occupation.

It would be unworthy of you to accept my unsupported word for this if you have any idea of dedicating yourself, your energies, your time, your education, and possibly your life's work to becoming a professional writer.

Therefore, it is necessary that I relate some facts from my personal experience with writers, editors, agents, and publishers to support my assertion that publishing and authorship are rock-ribbed institutions, not only here to stay but on a growth splurge that can only continue upward.

15

The only experiences I intend to draw upon are those that in my estimation are of interest and value to someone attracted to the writing of books or, possibly, to becoming an editor.

I do find myself apologizing that some of this material may appear to be an autobiography. It is not intended so. Rather, the first person, singular and the personal anecdote, seem the best human-interest devices with which to give a would-be writer an authentic and, hopefully, interesting picture of what actually happens, and has happened, in the world of the writers, editors, and publishers.

Every aspiring writer I have ever talked with has shown an overpowering curiosity about the publishing world; a huge hunger for facts about the business and the people in it. I consider satisfying some of that curiosity and hunger a most important, and pleasant, part of my responsibility.

It's true too I'm sure, that I want to brag a little, since it was my hand that held the torch of Fawcett's thousand-dollar bills that lit the fuse and set off a publishing explosion, worldwide and world-shaking.

Yes, Fawcett led this parade of record-breaking dollar payments made for paperback reprint rights. We were first to pay more than $100,000, first to pay more than a quarter-million dollars, first to pay more than a half-million for paperback reprint rights to a single book, first to make a million-dollar deal for reprint, and first to pay $1 million for reprint rights to one book. These payments were advances against royalties for American and Canadian rights only.

Since then Bantam has paid $1,850,000 as an advance against reprint royalties on a single book, *Ragtime*, by E. L. Doctorow, and before long more than $2 million will be paid for reprint rights to one book, as yet unpublished. It may be yours.

When it was decided Fawcett would go into the paperback field, my job was that of editorial director of the company. It was apparent to us as magazine publishers and distributors of magazines and books (including a line of paperback how-to books of our own and the paperback reprint line, Signet), that paperback books were becoming a booming industry. In 1950 we launched the first line of original paperbacks ever published—books not previously published in hardcover. We called the line of originals Gold Medal Books.

Gold Medal was quickly selling millions of books at twenty-five cents. But it was obvious to us that the real future in paperback publishing was that of publishing reprint editions of best-sellers by famous authors, so in 1955 we launched Crest and Premier books as reprint imprints. Signet went elsewhere for distribution and we concentrated on building our own lines of Gold Medal, Crest, and Premier.

From our experience with newsstand sales of magazines and distribution of Signet books, we knew, perhaps better than our competitors, how the reading public responded to "name" authors, and we set out to buy the best-selling books and famous authors for paperback reprint, no matter what the cost.

This decision was a company policy shared by Roger Fawcett, the man in charge, and his two brothers, Gordon and Roscoe. I was urged to spend whatever was necessary to get the best.

Any hardcover publisher with a best-seller learned quickly that Fawcett would top the bid of any competitor for a book we believed had outstanding sales potential. Then followed a period of several years in which our older entrenched paperback competitors were in shock, regularly refused to top the prices we bid, and let us walk off with the best-selling books by more than two dozen authors of proven ability. It was because of this foundation of authors, plus our experienced nationwide distribution system, that we quickly set new sales records for those authors whose books we published.

It is a fact that for a period of eighteen years, 1955-73, Fawcett set each record for the highest price paid for reprint rights for individual books, topping their own previous high in each case.

Thus we climbed very quickly to a paramount position in sales and suddenly became a leading paperback publisher, displacing competitors who had been in the business for more than a decade.

We got there with money, judgment as to what would sell, and luck. It is debatable whether the most important ingredient is the money, the judgment, or the luck, but we did spend money. In spending vast sums we forced our competitors to spend, and this spending of millions, where only thousands and hundreds had been spent before, put the whole book industry into orbit. This influx of millions of dollars of paperback reprint money is the development that has made books really BIG BUSINESS, an industry worthy of an author's time and energy. Because this is so important in the recent history of the industry's development, some additional circumstances must be related.

IT'S A BIG
MONEY BUSINESS

The first advance in the paperback industry that told trade publishers the paperback industry might be here to stay was $35,000 paid for reprint rights, against earned royalties, for *Naked and the Dead* by Norman Mailer. This record was broken in 1954 when Signet guaranteed $100,000 against royalties for paperback rights to *From Here to Eternity* by James Jones. This dramatic sum did send a shock wave through publishing circles, and most of the experts thought such an advance could not be earned back at a few-pennies-a-copy royalty; but they were wrong.

We started our campaign in 1955 by breaking the record $100,000 only modestly, by paying $101,505, an advance deliberately calculated to top the old record. The book *By Love Possessed* by James Gould Cozzens was definitely a "quality" work of fiction and one thought by many not suited to popular tastes.

We paid the new record-breaking price because the book was No. 1 as a hardcover best-seller on *The New York Times* list and because our experience as a distributor of paperback books and magazines gave us, I believe, a better understanding of the potential of paperback book sales at the newsstand than our competitors had. Few of our competitors had their own distribution system, in fact, only one, and that company's distribution was not as well established or as large. At any rate, our judgment paid off; we not only made a profit on *By Love Possessed*, but eventually paid considerably more than the $101,505 guarantee in royalties from sales.

In this period our energetic efforts to get books by established authors and our tradition-breaking high prices resulted in a rapid acceleration of prices paid at all levels for desirable books—best-sellers or not—and by all reprinters.

Suddenly routine mystery novels that had formerly sold for an advance against royalties of $3,500 or $2,000 were selling for $5,000, then $10,000 and higher. Inasmuch as these properties were, and still are, usually sold to the highest bidder by auction, all paperback publishers were paying more. In that period we created more than a small consternation in the business by paying $100,000 advance for *Lolita* by Vladimir Nabokov.

It wasn't until 1961 that we had to meet the challenge and again pay more for paperback reprint rights than had ever been paid before, and quite dramatically more! The book, *The Rise and Fall of the Third Reich* by William L. Shirer, and the price, $400,000 in pre-inflation dollars.

This price, nearly a half-million dollars for a reprint license on a serious work of contemporary history brought a loud collective gasp from the publishing industry. Simon & Schuster, from whom we bought the reprint rights, was widely congratulated for deciding not to publish *Rise and Fall* in their own paperback line, Pocket Books, but choosing to take our cash instead.

It is certainly an agreeable and comforting revelation that not only did Fawcett earn substantially more than the $400,000 advance for Simon and Schuster and Mr. Shirer, but we later paid Simon &

Schuster a large further advance to extend the license when the first license period lapsed.

So, with *Rise and Fall*, we had broken our own record of most-money paid, and this record held until we set a new record when we bought James A. Michener's *The Source* in 1965.

The facts concerning our successful effort to purchase *The Source* marked several firsts for the industry. Not only was the advance of $700,000 the largest ever paid, but we bought this book before it was published in hardcover. Generally at that period, books were put up for auction some time after publication; if a book was a best-seller it might not be sold for reprint until after it had been on the best-seller list for many months and thus demonstrated its worth to a reprinter.

Understandably, Bennett Cerf, president of Random House, was genuinely surprised and taken aback when I called on him in his office only a few days after galley proofs had been available to him with the announcement that I had come over to buy reprint rights to *The Source*.

Bennett was a hard man to fluster, as those of you who saw him on the TV show, *What's My Line?*, know; there was nothing in his demeanor to indicate he was put off balance by my brash announcement. Instead, he gave me the famous wide smile and said, "Oh, but you can't do that. All of Michener's reprints are done by Bantam. Besides, the book isn't printed yet."

My answer, twirling my mustache as befits the heavy when he notifies Little Nell the mortgage is overdue, was to tell him that I thought it was time Random House stopped selling their most desirable reprint properties to Bantam, frequently with no other reprinter having an opportunity to make an offer.

He agreed that Bantam had been in the position of favored purchaser and let me know he was enthusiastic about the large prices Fawcett was paying, some of which Random House had received for minor books. He also volunteered that Bantam had not been paying high enough prices and complimented Fawcett for what he called, "stirring up the bidding."

I refused to be distracted from my mission and reminded Bennett gently, while giving my mustache an extra twirl, of a circumstance I felt must, by this time, be somewhat embarrassing to Random House. This had to do with the interlocking ownership of Bantam Books by five large and powerful hardcover publishers (including Random House, Little, Brown & Co., and Charles Scribner's Sons). I even ventured an opinion that, under these circumstances, the Federal Trade Commission would probably look with less than enthusiasm on Bantam's acquiring more than what might be called "a fair share" of Random House books for reprint.

There was no mention of such horrid things as "unfair competition," "monopoly," or "restraint of trade," but Bennett admitted to some concern about the interlocking ownership of Bantam. Subsequently, Random House, Little, Brown & Co., and the others sold their stock in Bantam for a fine profit. A comment that must be made is that the fine old firm of Charles Scribner's Sons insisted on selling their Bantam stock at the price they originally paid for it, and, possibly because of a shadow that might be cast by the circumstances, thus refused to make a profit on the sale of their Bantam stock.

At this meeting Bennett gave me, somewhat reluctantly, a set of galleys for *The Source* but said he had already discussed the sale of the book with Bantam executives and they had indicated Bantam would pay more in advance money for *The Source* than they had paid for any other Michener book.

"How much?" I asked.

"Several hundred thousand dollars," he replied.

I told him I was leaving with my wife and daughter for a short vacation in Puerto Rico and that I would call him from the island after I had read the galley proofs to find out Bantam's top price. I told him flatly and firmly, and somewhat to his discomfort, that I expected to top Bantam's offer—no matter what it might be.

I started reading *The Source* on the plane and finished the awkward three-foot-long galleys the second day of my vacation, only slightly ahead of my wife and daughter. We formed a sort of assembly line as I passed each galley when I finished to my wife, an eager, enthusiastic reader, who in turn passed it to my appreciative sixteen-year-old daughter. (Strangely, I found out only last week that my wife still has the galleys carefully folded on a shelf in the attic).

I was enthralled with the magnificent book and willing to go to almost any lengths to obtain it, but I had no idea how much I might have to pay. Never before had I felt it necessary to consult Fawcett management on how much I might pay for a property, but recognizing that I would have to pay hugely, if indeed I could buy *The Source* at all, I decided to call Roger Fawcett.

Roger was in Rio de Janeiro, Brazil, and the only personal communication possible from Puerto Rico was the radio telephone through Miami. I placed the call and could vaguely hear the Miami operator. She was skeptical that the relayed voice transmission would work from Miami to Rio, but she would try.

Roger got on the phone quickly. I could barely hear his voice, and all I could distinguish was my name, Ralph, repeated over and over. He knew who was calling, where I was, and that there was some emergency, but I could not make clear that I wanted his permission to invest an unknown but large sum of money in the Michener book.

He did gather that I was asking permission to make a decision of some sort and I managed to hear his faint "Ok, ok, ok,!"

"That's the damndest OK I ever heard," I told my wife. "Roger said to go ahead, but he doesn't know what I asked him."

Nevertheless, with what I took to be his backing on anything I might have in mind, I felt reassured. I did wonder a bit whimsically if I could use his blanket okay to sell the Fawcett Company or to raise my salary.

So I called Bennett and asked him what was the best offer he had managed to elicit. He demurred and wouldn't tell me. The conversation ended with my telling him I felt entitled to top any offer he might get and that both his company and his author were entitled to learn how far I would go in my declared intention of paying more than any other reprinter. He said he would call back and he did.

Bennett considered himself a very honorable and fair man, and while he did not like the position he found himself in, he decided to settle it quickly. Instead of telling me how much Bantam would pay, and possibly letting me top that price, he chose to tell me how much Fawcett would have to pay before he would seriously consider our offer. If we chose to meet his price, Bantam would still have a chance to pay more and take the property. Thus acknowledging Bantam's rights as prior publisher.

I didn't like the cards I was holding under these circumstances, but at least I was now in a position to negotiate for the Michener book—and that represented progress over my position at the first meeting.

"What is your price?" I asked.

"You'll never pay it," he said. "You would have to guarantee us $700,000 against a royalty on sales of your edition at the royalty rate of twenty-five percent."

This did take my breath away!

I had done an elaborate set of estimate sheets, figuring at all conceivable sales levels the gross profit we might receive and how much we could afford to pay against estimated earnings in royalty. My figures indicated we had a gambling chance of breaking even if we paid the $700,000 advance, but the royalty of twenty-five percent was more than twice the reprint royalty rate usually paid, and this rate would effectively prevent earning a profit on our publication.

21

"I might meet the advance," I told him, "but the royalty rate is impossible."

"It's all or nothing," he replied.

"Will Bantam have to meet the twenty-five percent royalty rate as well as top the seven hundred thousand dollars if they beat us out?"

He replied, "Yes."

"Ok," I managed, in a voice that must have sounded "flutey," "We'll meet your terms."

"I'm sure you've got the book," he said, "but I'll call you back promptly and confirm." He did call back with the information that Bantam would not exceed our bid. We had the book!

News of the purchase was greeted with cheers by my wife and daughter, and I confess to a great surge of exultation.

My voice had not sounded "flutey," solely from the gamble I was taking with my employer's money. Sure, it was exciting and nerve-tingling to bet nearly three quarters of a million dollars on the paperback reprint sales potential of one book—more money than had ever before been paid for any kind of publishing rights for a single book!

But the greater thrill came from knowing we would own for reprint one of the most illuminating, moving, entertaining, and substantive books I had ever read. There was the warming knowledge, too, that this purchase would be the opening wedge for further purchase of Michener books if we could show the author and Random House how successful we could be in selling record-breaking numbers of our reprint edition. Subsequently we did buy each following new book this prolific author produced, including *Iberia*, *The Drifters*, and *Kent State*.

Then in 1973 when licenses earlier sold to Bantam on Michener's older books were expiring, Random House informed us that they and the author would like to negotiate an extension of these expiring licenses with Fawcett, and thus transfer all of Michener's books to us. This was when his newest book, *The Drifters*, was being published, and we were able to make a single purchase for reprint rights to *The Drifters* and all but one of the author's earlier books. Thus we added to our line those earlier great books of his, including *Tales of the South Pacific*, *Hawaii*, and *Caravans*.

The advance guarantee for purchase of this collection of jewels was—you guessed it—$1 million. The first million-dollar deal in publishing!

As part of this whole negotiation I should mention that some years after this, when the original reprint license on *The Source* expired, I took our accounting books to Random House and showed Bennett Cerf that we had made no profit on this book, in spite of a very large copy sale, and suggested a reduction of the ruinous twenty-five percent royalty. It is a tribute to the essential fairness of Random House and the author, that this royalty rate was then reduced.

The latest chapter of this record-breaking affair between Fawcett, Random House, and Michener was written when Fawcett Publisher Leona Nevler bought paperback reprint rights to the newest Michener best-seller, *Centennial,* for a guarantee $1 million against royalty earned.

This purchase, in spite of any conflicting publicity-spawned claims by other reprinters, is the first time a million dollars was specifically guaranteed for reprint rights to a single book.

BEING RICH NEED NOT BE BAD

Why am I telling you all this behind-the-scenes information, with so much emphasis on money? Only a few years ago, when publishing was so frequently conceded to be a paragon of noncommercial gentility, such an emphasis would not have been possible. Had it been possible, it would have been frowned upon!

But times have changed. If it is not now clear to you, it will be as we go along that money, and chiefly the large sums paid for reprint rights to books by big-name authors, has turned the publishing industry topsy-turvy. Now writers are less likely to be living in traditional garrets than in country estates, duplexes on Park Avenue, haciendas in Spain, sixty-foot schooners, or fifty thousand dollar mobile homes.

And the reason I'm piling up all these gold pieces before your eyes is to clearly inform you what has happened to the publishing business because of paperback reprints and to tell all who will listen that it is the big prices paid for the *author's* work that has brought significant change to the industry.

I believe, too, that while the industry's story could be told with statistics, and I will throw in some of those by and by, the actual happenings and anecdotes of people concerned will give you a better knowledge of the industry you might choose to ally yourself with.

Hopefully, it is clear to all that our record of paying higher prices than our competitors for the best-sellers we wanted for the eighteen-year period, 1955-73, was not for the purpose of setting and breaking records. Indeed, we were not anxious for the news of the big prices we paid to get out in the trade for the accelerating effect such news would have on all purchase of reprint rights. But the word did get out, as hardcover houses found this new, very substantial source of revenue—usually split fifty-fifty between author and hardcover publisher at that period—most welcome. Indeed, the profit the hardcover publisher realized from his share of reprint royalty was frequently much more than he made on the hardcover sale of his edition. Or the profit from the reprint sale turned a loss on the book, as originally published in hardcover, into a profit.

It is a peculiar fact of this peculiar business, book publishing, that even today, most hardcover publishers would be losing money on their trade book division if it were not for their receiving a share of the paperback reprint revenue.

We at Fawcett were earning a profit, too, but not as large as the publicity given to our numerous purchases for big money would indicate. Actually, at that time we were making a profit on each of the books on which we had advanced $200,000 or more, because most of the books at this level had proven themselves in hardcover. We did fail to earn the advance, and lost rather substantially, on a number of books whose advances were below the $200,000 level, including books at $150,000, $100,000, $50,000, and even $25,000. These books, for the most part, had not proven themselves as trade books when we bought them, and our judgment of their sales potential was too enthusiastic or just plain wrong. I won't list any of the losing titles, because to do so would embarrass the authors and/or me.

At that time Fawcett's contractual obligations amounted to more than $12 million in guaranteed advances against earned royalties, and today it is larger. All of this money was being paid to trade book publishers to be divided with their authors.

This influx of millions of dollars of new money into the publishing industry from paperback publishers could be expected to have some dramatic effects, and it did. And so that you, as an author-to-be, may be properly informed, I want to define and interpret the financial situation that resulted in all these "advances against royalties," I have been mentioning.

It is probably widely known that when an author licenses his manuscript to a hardcover publisher, he is given an advance or "down payment," usually of several thousand dollars. This advance is considered to be payment against what the book may earn for the author at a royalty rate agreed upon between publisher and author. If the rate is ten percent and the book sells for ten dollars, the author will earn one dollar for each copy sold. He may get $5,000 in advance—or less or more—but he will not get any more earnings from that book until his earnings at the agreed-upon royalty rate exceed what has been paid in advance.

The author will get royalty statements from his publisher twice a year: one with a detailed sales estimate for the period ending June 30, and the second with a similar estimate to December 31. These statements follow the end date period by about three months. Since they are estimates, and not actual reports of sales made, an author may not expect to get further payment over his advance on the first or the second royalty statement after publication, unless the book is a proven best-seller.

The publisher would like to pay faster, and he would if he knew how many copies had been actually bought by readers, but he doesn't know. The publishing industry, both hardcover and soft, runs on what is commonly called a "fully returnable" basis. Meaning that the retailer, jobber, or wholesaler can return any unsold books for credit, and the industry is so chaotic that it is not altogether unusual for a dealer to order fifty copies of the very title he had returned forty copies of unsold the previous day. The dealer can do this, of course, at no risk to himself. Hence, the publisher cannot make an accurate estimate of his sales for many months, or even years, after publication of a title. It amuses me that British publishers call this system, "See safe," which they interpret to their trade as "seeing the retailer safe from loss" and which the author interprets as seeing the publisher safe. Be that as it may, the author must wait for any further payment beyond his advance until sales are known.

But not always. When we started Gold Medal—the first paperback line of original books, not reprints—I developed a system of paying royalty on number of copies printed, rather than on copies sold; meaning that the author was paid any money due him over the advance as soon as the book was printed, or "within thirty days thereafter," as the contract states.

It works this way: Suppose Gold Medal buys a novel from you for an advance payment of $3,000, the advance to be against a royalty of five percent of cover price. This royalty rate is negotiable—high if we think we can sell a lot of copies, lower if we have a contrary view. Let's assume the book has a cover price of 95 cents. Thus at a five percent royalty rate, we will pay you $.0475 per copy printed. In case decimals are not your long suit, that is four-and-three-quarters cents for every copy printed.

If the first printing is 100,000, and that is a "low-reasonable" estimate, you will be entitled to a total of $4,750—$3,000 of which has already been given you as an advance. So within 30 days after that book is printed and we have the "manufactured count" from the printer, we will send you a check for the balance of $1,750. If the first printing is 200,000, we will send an additional check for $6,500. In the years to come, on any additional printings, more royalties will be sent you as due.

The above is merely for explanation purposes, but it is a fact that some Gold Medal first printings have exceeded 500,000 copies and that many of the Fawcett original books have sold in excess of 1,000,000 copies.

Each of the many westerns Gold Medal has published by Louis L'Amour, prior to those published in 1974, has sold over 1,000,000 copies and is still actively reprinted. Those published since 1974 will also sell in that range.

John D. MacDonald is another author who has found the original paperback field, and royalty paid on printing, to his liking. He has more than 50 books in print with Gold Medal, including 17 in the famous "Travis McGee" series. John has more than 52,000,000 copies of his Gold Medal books in print on which royalty has been paid. He was attracted to the theory of original publication in paperback because he did not like splitting his paperback royalties with a hardcover publisher—a conclusion reached possibly as a result of his being a graduate of the Harvard Business School. Currently he is grinning hugely because a hardcover publisher, E. P. Dutton, is successfully republishing in hardcover the Travis McGee books formerly published in paperback by Gold Medal. John is grinning because he is now getting all the royalty, hard and soft-cover, with no publisher sharing it.

The successful following of the paperback edition with a hard-cover edition is another evidence of the revolution in publishing; all of it sponsored and initiated by more money for the authors and because paperbacks have found more readers for lower-price books.

But back to the author-royalty situation, and one which will shed more light on John D.'s decision.

Hardcover publishers, frequently identified as "trade book publishers," believe they are entitled to some of the money earned by an author's work when republished in the paperback edition. They also are accustomed to receiving a portion of the other revenues received for use of the author's work. These monies are paid for secondary or, more commonly, "subsidiary rights." These rights may include, in addition to paperback reprint revenue, money received for sale of foreign language rights, motion picture rights, theatrical performing rights, magazine reprint rights, recording rights (usually for instructional records or tapes, or in braille), anthology rights (the use of portions of the whole in other books), book club rights, and such rights as are required for use in the famous Reader's Digest Condensed Books.

Just so no potential sources of earnings are bypassed, the original hardcover contract may contain a claim by the publisher for a portion of the author's earnings from presently unknown sources. The contract may read, "for use of this work in any form in any medium not currently or hitherto known, but including use by devices or inventions that may occur during the period of this license."

So, should some space age invention come along permitting the capsulating of the author's work and shooting same into an individual's head through his nose, rather than reaching him through the conventional ear or eye, the trade publisher is cut in for a piece of the action.

The basic information I am giving you about authors' contracts should also include the admonition that when you write your book, and it is suddenly contract time, have your contract approved by an agent or a lawyer and be sure you understand every word in it.

It is unlikely any publisher will try to do you dirt (the Authors League has pretty well led to the universal use of a semi-standard contract), but you need the protection of legal or expert advice in signing your first contract because the stars in your eyes and the bells in your ears may lead to a degree of confusion on your part.

In addition to provision for payment and license of rights your contract will specify term or length of the contract. This period is usually for the full term of the copyright, until 1976 a period of twenty-eight years that could be extended to a maximum of fifty-six by renewing the copyright for a second twenty-eight-year period. Provision is made in the contract for returning all publishing rights to the author if the work is no longer in print prior to expiration of the copyright.

There is now cause for authors to celebrate a new and altogether better copyright law obtained as a result of many years of hard work on the part of the Authors League, the Publishers Association and other interested parties.

Simply stated the new law says that a manuscript of your authorship is considered your exclusive property under statutory law until such a time as it is published. Once your material is published, a copyright notice printed on it, and the copyright registered with the U.S. Copyright Office, the copyright, and thus ownership, will be in force for the entire period of your life plus fifty years. If the work is registered in the names of two persons the copyright will be in effect until fifty years after the death of the last survivor. Under this new law the length of the copyright is substantially extended and gives a copyrighted work that is still earning money the aura of an estate that can be willed to heirs for a meaningful period. Or, if all rights are sold, the value of the work will be enhanced because the rights to the property will belong to the purchaser longer than they would under the old law. Under the earlier law the copyright holder lost all ownership when the work went into public domain after a maximum of fifty-six years.

Further changes have been made to the copyright owner's advantage for a work presently in copyright under the old law. For example, if you now own the copyright on a book already in copyright in its first or second twenty-eight-year period, the copyright is considered extended for a period of 75 years from date of its first publication.

Copyright is considered the best proof of ownership by our courts and you should expect that the copyright of your book is to be made in your name or in the name of the person or corporation you have reason to identify as the owner of your work.

Today it is rare if a hardcover publisher gets more than fifteen percent of any movie sale revenue; more frequently, they get none. The largest single subsidiary sale revenue comes from the paperback publication and, until quite recently, the hardcover publisher always received fifty percent of the paperback reprint earnings.

The publishing revolution has changed that. Now trade publishers are willing, under some circumstances, to negotiate for a smaller than fifty percent share of paperback revenues. It is quite common for a successful author to receive sixty percent of his paperback revenue, his hardcover publisher forty percent. It is a fact that some of the very popular authors are giving up to the hardcover publisher as little as twenty percent, ten percent, five percent, or nothing at all in some exceptional cases.

Such an "exceptional" case, according to trade gossip, concerns the famous best-seller, *Everything You Always Wanted to Know About Sex but Were Afraid to Ask,* by Dr. Reuben. This book was actually contracted for and written under the supervision of Bantam, the reprint publisher. When the manuscript was finished and it became apparent to the highly perceptive Bantam management that they had a real blockbuster, it also occurred to them that the book would sell hugely in hardcover at a very high cover price. Such a hardcover sale would guarantee that the paperback sale a year or so later would be maximum, because trade publication gives stature and gets more reviews than does original paperback. Also, because of the then daring and sexually frank content of the book, hardcover publication would be easier to defend legally if censorship developed.

"So," said the Bantam executives among themselves, "perhaps we can find a trade publisher who will bring out this splendid book and not take any paperback royalty," leaving more for the author and Bantam, though not necessarily in that order.

David McKay Co., Inc., a large and successful trade publisher, then under the managership of Kennett Rawson, agreed to publish the hardcover edition at an agreed-upon royalty to be paid by them to Bantam, who in turn paid some unknown portion to the author or authors. Persons at McKay have made noises that might be interpreted as indicating McKay is getting some very small portion of the paperback royalties and, if so, that is indeed what might be called "the old switcheroo."

Chances are McKay got no part of the paperback earnings and is content with their earnings from the hardcover book, which has sold over a million copies.

There is another and better substantiated case to the royalty details, also instigated by Bantam—certainly the most energetic and innovative of the paperback houses—which concerns not splitting paperback royalties with hardcover publishers if it can be avoided. This has to do with the author, Jacqueline Susann, who was brought out of obscurity as an author by Bernard Geis Associates, who published her first two books. This smallish firm leaped into prominence with a list of best-sellers by such authors as Helen Gurley Brown (author of the famous *Sex and the Single Girl*), Art Linkletter, Groucho Marx, President Truman, Vincent Price, and others.

The late Miss Susann, a former Hollywood bit player, submitted her first book—a true account of life with her pet poodle—to Mr. Geis. After considerable rewriting and revision under his direction, it was published as *Every Night, Josephine!* and became a minor best-seller, reaching No. 10 on *Time* magazine's list. Not a little of this book's success (and that of her subsequent books) was due to the highly professional publicity efforts of her husband, Irving Mansfield, an acknowledged expert in the craft of creating public interest in books, authors, movie stars, and even poodles.

Mr. Geis admits to some surprise when Miss Susann presented him with the manuscript of a second book, a novel. His editorial staff reported to him that the book was junk—amateurish and unpublishable. Bernie read it and seemed to detect a quality that might be counted upon to attract and hold readers, a quality sometimes spelled s-e-x. He has since been quoted as saying of the manuscript, "Reading that first draft was like listening in on a bugged bedroom in which two extrovert couples were in bed together."

That first version, as submitted, had even more than the usual number of first-novel gaffs—characters suddenly dropping out of sight because the author had unwittingly changed their names, flowery descriptions, dialogue more wooden than wonderful, and repeatedly characterized by "he said, she said." But the manuscript was hard to put down. It reflected a pronounced degree of reality, possibly because the book's fictional characters may have been thinly disguised portraits of real persons—stars of the Hollywood film world.

So, as men will when in doubt, Mr. Geis took the manuscript home for his wife's reaction. Darlene Geis, a professional editor in the field of art books and an author, urged him to make the effort to see if Miss Susann, with assistance, could rewrite and make the "novel" something salable.

The next step was for Bernie to hand it to his top editor, Don Preston, with the instruction, "Don't come back to the office until this manuscript is publishable."

Six weeks later, after intensive collaboration and rewriting by Miss Susann and Mr. Preston, *Valley of the Dolls* was ready for publication. The book, under an intensive publicity campaign developed by Bernie and Irving Mansfield, with whirlwind public appearances on leading TV shows by Miss Susann, became a huge, much talked about best-seller. Miss Susann became an overnight celebrity—a role she enjoyed as much as she enjoyed being called an "author."

Paperback reprint rights went to Bantam for $125,000 (Fawcett goofed) and the book eventually earned more than $1 million in reprint royalties for the author and for Mr. Geis.

But the lady who had been so pleased when Bernie Geis published her first book about her poodle and expressed her gratitude when he and his editor worked with her to make her first novel publishable was persuaded, by what influences I do not know, that her monetary situation would be much more attractive if she did not share the reprint royalty on her next book with hardcover publisher Geis, but were to keep all of it for herself.

What went on behind the scenes is widely surmised, but what is actually known is that Bantam bought Miss Susann's original contract from Mr. Geis. The contract was sold reluctantly, containing as it did an option for the author's next novel, which proved to be the very successful *The Love Machine*. This book was published in its hardcover trade edition by Simon and Schuster, without their getting reprint royalties from Bantam. Thus Miss Susann found herself on the road to what is called "the best of everything." She did not share her paperback or hardcover royalties with any publisher.

The Love Machine became a best-seller, too, but for some reason Bantam, who continued as her publisher of record, placed her third best-seller, *Once Is Not Enough*, with trade publisher, William Morrow. Larry Hughes, president of that company, expressed satisfaction with the profit made from the sale of more than two hundred thousand hardcover copies, "and a very small percentage of the paperback royalty."

Such maneuvering would never have been possible without the large paperback earnings. Increasingly the larger selling authors are trying to find ways to get more of the total book revenue, hard and softcover, for themselves.

I don't intend to moralize about this situation but, objectively, I do not approve of publishers raiding the lists of other publishers, and particularly do I find it against my sense of fairness when paperback reprinters take authors from hardcover houses, then license the author's work back to a hardcover house, as just reported. Sure, if the author is a genuine, guaranteed best-seller he may make more money, at least for a time, and I do like to see authors get money. It is a fact, though, that the author doesn't get to the best-seller stature that makes him coveted by other publishers—trade or paperback —by himself. The author owes some of his success, be it a large or small portion, to his original publisher and editor. The author at no time could have made his success by himself, even though it is his product that is the single most valuable contribution.

No, the author is not the *whole* story. He is frequently more dependent on his editor than he will admit or even know. With the sensitivity authors are famous for, he responds most productively to a warm relationship of mutual trust and admiration with his publisher, his editor, and with his agent, if he has one. The kind of relationship I refer to is illustrated by the instance when Random House and James Michener demonstrated a willingness to adjust the too-high royalty rate they originally exacted for *The Source* as the price of moving the author to Fawcett. I look upon this incident as an extension of the author-editor-publisher relationship that is exemplified in James Michener's rapport with Random House and his longtime friend, counselor, and editor there, Albert Erskine. I'd better point out, too, that in the real sense I did not "raid" Bantam for *The Source*. At that time the multiple ownership of Bantam by a group of trade publishers was resulting in an indefensible situation in which Bantam, if they were given any degree of preferential treatment in purchasing reprint rights from authors controlled by these publishers, was possibly getting them too cheaply and at the expense of the authors.

As reported earlier Random House and the other trade publisher owners sold their interests in Bantam, because the ownership of a reprint house by a group of competing hardcover publishers was of doubtful legality and represented a situation to which authors and agents could object.

HOW MUCH AM I BID?

The sale of reprint and other subsidiary rights is so important and of such selfish monetary interest that you are entitled to an explanation of the practices of the trade concerning these matters.

It may be that you have some knowledge of these affairs, but such knowledge may be incomplete. Indeed there are some innovations creeping in to what, until recently, were accepted as rather rigid trade practices in the sale of publishing rights. The fact is these "standard trade practices" have been badly bent and even completely disregarded in some instances as the competitive scramble for the author's manuscript has intensified. This scramble, of course, is because the author's work has demonstrated dramatically that it can earn large sums of money

When an American hardcover publisher sends you that glad news, "we want to buy your book," the publisher is usually telling you that he wants to buy the rights to publish, or license publication, of your book worldwide and in all languages.

He expects to publish in the United States, sell foreign language rights around the world, sell other subsidiary rights, and retain a commission for these services.

If your American hardcover publisher does not have a foreign rights department, he may buy "worldwide English language rights," or only "English language rights for the United States and Canada."

If he buys "worldwide English language rights," he will license rights to a British publisher for publication of the work in Great Britain and what is sometimes referred to as "the British Commonwealth." This territory consists of the British Isles and various areas where British influence is of long-standing, such as Australia, New Zealand, and South Africa.

The larger American publishers are equipped to handle sales of worldwide rights in all languages, and the author of a first novel or first book is probably better off permitting his hardcover publisher to handle sales of foreign rights. If he is not equipped to handle these sales it will be necessary to obtain an agent to handle the matter for you.

If you have been fortunate enough to have an agent when you made your first sale, the agent will decide whether to permit the hardcover publisher to sell foreign rights. If big money is at stake for these foreign rights, the agent will insist on handling the sales abroad himself, and thus will save you the money you might have had to pay the American publisher for this service.

There are other subsidiary rights which your American hardcover publisher will insist upon handling for you. These may include book club rights, magazine or newspaper serialization, motion picture, TV, and radio rights, as well as the all-important paperback reprint rights.

Unless you have an agent it is best that your hardcover publisher handle all these rights for you. Money paid for these rights is frequently substantial—you can expect to share book club payments fifty-fifty, with book club advances sometimes exceeding fifty thousand dollars. You may also expect to share magazine and newspaper serialization revenues fifty-fifty.

If your publisher handles motion picture rights, his share should not exceed fifteen percent, or twenty-five percent at the most. In years past the book publisher would get fifty percent or even more on such revenues, but not any more. If you are represented by an agent, the agent will handle the sale of motion picture rights, and the publisher will probably get no share.

Earlier I mentioned that innovations are creeping in and changing what used to be accepted trade practices concerning the sale of the many rights to an author's work. Not all of these changes are to the publisher's advantage.

One of the situations not to the publisher's advantage is the increasingly frequent submission of an author's unpublished manuscript to several hardcover publishers simultaneously and the soliciting of competitive bids for the rights to publish.

Until very recently none of the larger, more reputable publishers would participate in such a competitive scramble for an author's work. "Multiple submission," as it was called, was not tolerated, and manuscripts known to have been submitted to more than one publisher at the same time were returned unread.

This policy is still rather generally followed, unless the author is a proven big money earner and is suddenly free of contractual obligations with his established publisher. Under these favorable circumstances (favorable for the author, that is) the agent has been known to whip out a single-paragraph letter to a select group of major publishers with an invitation for those interested to come up with a suggestion for front money and royalty terms for "Mr. Best-seller's next book-length manuscript." The highest bidder will get the work and possibly the opportunity to purchase Mr. Best-seller's second and third work as well.

When this marketing innovation first happened, publishers' screams exceeded the decible level of the supersonic Concorde. There was talk of outlawing the agent who first proposed such a revolutionary invasion of the publisher's right to negotiate purchase of an author's work without competitive pressure and bidding from some brother publisher who might want to pay a higher price for the manuscript.

It just so happens that it was the hardcover publisher who first pulled this trigger and now finds himself staring into the muzzle of his own gun.

This oblique reference is to the suicidal fact that it was the hardcover publisher who loosed the "multiple submission" scourge and now complains that it is a wolf eating at his vitals.

I am referring to the time, not so long ago, when hardcover publishers got as much as fifty percent of money received for motion picture sales.

Then it was the motion picture producers who expected a chance to buy a story property without multiple submission or an auction.

But one day the hardcover publishers changed the procedure and sent the manuscripts abroad in a regular blizzard to all motion picture producers. "Let's have your best offer," said the publishers, "and we shall see if your competitor will pay more. If so, we'll be back for your best offer."

Today it is the hardcover publisher who in similar fashion gives all reprint publishers a chance to outbid all of their competitors for rights to an author's work, unless the reprinter has a contractual arrangement or "option," for the new work as a result of the reprinter having published the author's previous work.

Actually, such options are usually quite loose and state something to the effect, that "the reprinter shall be entitled to negotiate for the other's next book, at terms to be arranged."

Thus if the hardcover publisher believes he can get a larger advance from a reprinter other than the one who published the author's previous work, the hardcover publisher may refuse to accept the original reprinter's terms and send the manuscript out for bids from all reprinters.

This, of course, is nothing else than the "multiple submission" the hardcover publisher objects to when he is subjected to competitive bidding for an author's manuscript. It is the identical high-pressure tactic the hardcover publisher subjected the moviemakers to in these early days. As such it can be called retribution.

The whole "round and round we go" situation can also be defined as the competitive way. When more than one party desires a property—be it manuscript, diamond, or rare stamp—the price goes up and the bidding is intense. Today, authors and their salable manuscripts are among the most desired of the world's precious objects.

Does this bring a glow to you—that your manuscript may be the object of push-pull and high prices as a result of competitive bidding?

If so, don't get carried away. Because if you, as yet an unknown author, attempt to submit your manuscript to more than one publisher at a time, your manuscript will be returned unread.

The unwillingness of a publisher to spend his time reading a manuscript from an unknown, unproven author when the publisher is aware that the manuscript has been submitted simultaneously to other publishers is completely understandable and correct.

It would be uneconomical and unreasonable for a publisher's editors to go through the process of reading, evaluating, and detailing suggested changes and revision that invariably are necessary in first manuscripts, and then find that other publishers are in a competition to attempt to make a successful writer from a tyro.

No, until you have made the first sale and had that first book published, don't worry about whether you got the absolute final advance dollar possible for your brainchild.

It is my observation that authors who concentrate on their writing and trust their publishers to concentrate on doing their job in a professional manner will profit most. Publishers are trustworthy. Blessed indeed is the author who knows his publisher to be his friend and his partner, and blessed the author whose agent handles the business matters smoothly and well.

WHAT HAPPENS WHEN YOUR BOOK IS PUBLISHED?

When your book is purchased by a trade publisher, advance proofs or Xerox copies of your manuscript will be submitted to all reprinters, whether they have expressed active interest or not, with the information that on a certain day, possibly three weeks hence, bids will be received and the reprint purchaser named.

Several copies of the advance proofs are received in each reprinter's office and are immediately assigned for staff readings. Some outside reader, with special expertise on the book's subject matter, may be chosen and perhaps two staff editors will be given reading copies.

Within a few days (or even a few hours, as editors are famed for their reading speed, in fact, some of them are capable of reading three or more novels in a single evening) reports will be written by each reader and forwarded to the editor in chief and, possibly, the publisher. If these reports are favorable or in any degree enthusiastic, the editor and, possibly, the publisher, will read the book (if he or she has not already done so). Editors in chief and most publishers are constant nonstop readers, never willing to leave the office without something to read for possible purchase, and are in the habit of picking up proof copies of new books the day they arrive. So they may have read your book by the time the readers' reports come in.

Nevertheless, except in those houses whose publishers or top editors choose books by supernatural divination or the whisper of Oracles ("I just know it will sell"), the reports are carefully studied. If you have written other books, the sales records and reviews of those books are also inspected, and a decision is made as to whether or not to enter the bidding fray. Sometimes this decision is made by committee, but more often it is made by the top editor. In making the decision he has many factors in mind: whether this book and you, as an author, complement the publisher's line, whether his company can achieve maximum sales for your book (for it is a fact that a paperback publisher who has had outstanding success with a certain category of book can frequently sell more similar books than can another). Other factors might be as far afield as your, possibly, having at some former time made off with the editor's girl friend or boyfriend; then, depending on the circumstances, the editor's bidding might be influenced by gratitude or jealousy.

Once the decision is made to bid and the book is greatly desired by the editor, he may call up the seller as soon as possible and inquire if the trade publisher will accept a "topping" bid. If "topping" is granted by the seller, the would-be purchaser has the option to "top" the highest competitive bid received by ten percent.

Thus, if topping is granted to a reprinter and the highest bid the seller can whip up from other reprinters is $100,000, the topper can claim the property for $110,000. In case topping is granted, all the bidders are informed when bids are asked for that some reprinter has this favored position. There is sometimes a tendency for topping to slow down the bidding and keep it at a level lower than might be attained if bidding were unrestricted. There have also been instances when some vengeance-seeking reprinter will take what chances are implied in bidding the property up because he knows that one of his rival reprinters, who has topping in this instance, is determined to get the property. In these instances the vengeance seeker is out to stick his rival with the property at the highest possible price, thus glutting his rival's inventory, reducing his operating cash, and keeping him out of bidding competition for other more desirable upcoming properties.

It wasn't always such a shoot-them-down business—not until it became common knowledge that the public would buy almost unlimited quantities of books they desired to read; such as *The God-father*, a Fawcett reprint and today the largest-selling novel ever published, with a total sale, in the English language alone, that exceeds 15 million copies.

In earlier and less competitive days there was no uniform method used by trade publishers to dispose of reprint rights. Sometimes a mere phone call and an expression by the reprinter of a desire to publish the trade publisher's new book would result in a purchase made over the phone at a price mutually acceptable, and at what were called "standard royalties."

In the very early days the trade house might dispose of reprint rights and then inform the author they had been sold, but no longer! The book contracts usually give authors approval of reprint sales, as to purchaser, royalty, terms, and all other details.

With book purchasers ready to pay out millions for books they want to read, with agents getting ten percent of authors' earnings, with reprinters demonstrating they will pay big money for salable properties (sometimes just to keep their competitive standing) the market is very lively indeed. It has now reached the point where several minor reprinters have been forced out of business, but those who remain are selling more books than ever, but for less profit than they were accustomed to.

So stimulated has the business become that the subsidiary

rights editor, the employee in charge of selling reprint rights, is now a separate category of "editor" in every trade house except the very smallest. His, or her, position in the house is considered so important that the subsidiary editor is among the highest paid editors on the staff and, in at least one instance, has a salary augmented by a percentage of the total advance payment or guarantee he has been able to squeeze out of the reprint purchaser.

The inferences of this situation are not healthy for the author, the reprinter, the trade publisher, or even the agent. A subsidiary rights editor spurred on by a commission paid out of the amount of advance he can wring out of a reprinter is part of a selfishly motivated chain of events that has built-in whiplash. Pressures are exerted all along the line of a type likely to foster eventual wide-open bidding among hardcover houses for unpublished properties, as is the case with reprint auctions today.

Not every publisher wants to wring the last penny of advance from the reprinter; neither does every agent or every author. Some are showing relatively more interest in contract details other than the advance. Such details include the royalty rate and the experience and proven efficiency of the reprinter's circulation department. In not pushing for the last possible dime the author and hardcover publisher are not putting themselves in an "unfriendly" situation of having profited from the reprinter's unprofitable venture.

There is increasing evidence that more and more trade houses are reaching the conclusion that their and the author's best interests are not well-served in settling simply for the top dollar.

How is a reprint auction conducted?

Over the telephone. In past years there were a few sales on the basis of sealed bids, but no more.

On deadline day the reprinter interested in purchasing a submitted property phones in his offer usually near the deadline, which is commonly 5:00 P.M. If a higher offer has already been received by the seller, he will usually tell the bidder, giving him a chance to increase his bid on the phone.

The bidder is not told at that point what the top bid is. Instead the seller will start a whirling sensation in the bidder's cranium by saying, "Thank you very much for your interest, old chap, but the bid you offer will not put you in the finals."

Then follows a cautious mating dance. The bidder says, "Will another ten thousand dollars put me in?" and so on, until the bidder is in a position to be one of the finalists or has dropped out of the competition.

The last round of bidding among finalists may take days or

weeks, as the sparring opponents strive to come up with more money and inspired offers of superior treatment for the author's work. In the end the book would go to the reprinter making the best money offer. Today this isn't always so.

Once, and only once, did I lose a book on which I had bid more, some $12,000 more, than my competitor. The author's hardcover publisher, who assumed the author would take our higher bid, had already indicated we would get the property. But the author insisted that his books go to the reprinter who had bid less, although the decision might cost him fifty percent of the difference, or about $6,000. It would also cost the hardcover house that much if the book did not earn more than the guarantee. So with his publisher's permission I drove a fast 150 miles to reason personally with the male author of this best-seller, but no dice. He remained stubborn.

Later I was told the author had promised a girl friend on my competitor's staff that he would sell the book, his first, to her firm. Sex, insanity, or just $12,000 worth of old-fashioned romantic courtesy? I never found out.

Here is a thought-provoking fact in the current practice of the auction procedure that adds an atmosphere of Russian roulette:

With hardly any exceptions the trade houses are selling reprint rights to every new book on their list before the hardcover edition is published—frequently a year before the hardcover is published, sometimes two years, and sometimes before the book is written!

Thus the reprint publisher has no information as to the public reaction to the hardcover. Will the book, when published, sell hugely or fail? All he has to base his bid on is the judgment—or guess—of his staff and himself after they have read the manuscript, if there is one to read.

A talented, experienced editor, W. C. Lengel, then editor in chief of Crest and Gold Medal, summed up this situation: "Buying an unpublished book for reprint is like playing poker in the dark —without a deck of cards."

As might be expected with such large sums being bid in such an informal atmosphere as a telephone auction, there has been some cheating. Probably not much, but some, and enough so the paperback reprinters have met together to discuss this problem. At the meeting an agreement was reached among them that if any suspicious circumstance develops in connection with the auction of any book, then the bidders will get together after the sale and compare notes on who bid how much.

This agreement has pretty effectively prevented the possibility of crookedness. Before this agreement to compare bids after the auction, there was one proven case in which a hardcover publisher was persuaded to refund forty thousand dollars which his overenthusiastic rights editor had dragged out of a reprinter by insinuating there was a larger bid in hand than he really had.

There have been other sharp practices, too, including a number of instances in which reprinters were conned into raising their own bid by the rights editor murmuring confidentially: "Another ten thousand dollars will get you the book, I'm pretty sure," when all the time it was the eager bidder on the phone who had already bid the top price. Thus he was raising his own bid.

These blind bidding circumstances are not without instances of wry amusement. For example, in some cases the first indication the trade publisher has that the book he is offering is a potential bestseller is when a reprinter proves willing to pay an advance of $100,000, or even $400,000, for a book the trade publisher had expected to bring only $10,000.

When this happens, and it has happened frequently, the trade publisher gathers his staff around him while he utters his version of the exclamation: "What hath God wrought?" Or maybe, "Why in Christ's sake didn't somebody around here know the book was that good?" (For hardcover publishers do value reprinter's judgment.) "Now let's make some advertising and publicity plans. We can't just sit back and take the reprinter's money without giving the book a push."

In one such instance there is reason to believe a book almost sold for reprint for an advance payment of $50,000, but in a belated bidding situation sold for more than $400,000 and earned over $2 million for the author. A bit later I shall tell you more of this author-heartening instance as part of my efforts to convince the able and worthy among you that authorship is the essential part of a profitable, satisfying, and exciting profession. More exciting than fishing! At its highest level of financial reward it is very likely to spoil you forever for low-stake poker.

EVERYBODY MAKES MISTAKES

Certainly the industry is filled with both success stories and failures, instances when agents made right moves for their clients and wrong moves: Times when publishers overextended themselves in meeting an author's demands and suffered losses; times when a manuscript purchased for an insignificant advance went on to top the best-seller list, as did *Jonathan Livingston Seagull* by Richard Bach, a success that continues to baffle the industry and to remind all in it that the totally unexpected success is frequent enough that every submitted manuscript should be given the most careful scrutiny.

Agents and publishers are not the only ones capable of *le grand goof*. Authors err, too, and one not uncommon instance is when an author insists on changing publishers in a situation where the partnership has been working very well.

One author who made such a decision is Richard Prather, originator of an extremely successful series featuring the fictional detective, Shell Scott. This once-popular series sold millions of books in Gold Medal editions.

Dick made his first book sale to Fawcett while employed as a clerk in a military training base, allegedly at a wage of fifty dollars a week. The submitted manuscript was recognized as having merit by editor Richard Carroll. Correspondence between editor and author led to rewriting and revision and, eventually, to our purchasing the manuscript: a Spillane-type action detective-mystery featuring the unique character, Shell Scott.

Instead of a deadly serious detective hero, Prather had come up with an amusing shamus who mixed laughs with violence and a degree of sex that was considered titillating in the 1950s. One very successful book followed another in the series, edition following edition, and soon Mr. Prather's income permitted him to buy a dramatic Hawaiian-California-type house, picturesquely perched on the side of a mountain overlooking the Pacific Ocean. On each of the frequent trips our editors or I made to the coast, meetings both social and for business reasons, were held with Richard and his beautiful wife, Tina.

More than a dozen books had been published and the series pushed to ever-increasing sales, with Fawcett giving the author increases in his royalty rate as his success grew. On each trip to California Dick was always profuse in thanking each of us for our part in his success, and he swore undying fealty.

Then it happened. I got a call from Prather's agent, Scott Meredith. He wanted to see me on something "important."

Once in my office, Scott came quickly to the point. One of our competitors, unnamed at that point, had made a very substantial bid for Dick's upcoming books, and Dick was inclined to move unless Fawcett improved the present arrangements to a degree that would match the new offer. "I have not suggested Dick accept the offer," said Scott. "I have told him it is a decision *he* will have to make."

"What is the offer?" (I should have known!)

"One million dollars," came the magic answer.

Mr. Meredith went on to explain the details, while I reflected that the agent's commission was a tidy $100,000, at the usual agent's commission of ten percent. Certainly sporting of him not to recommend acceptance by his client and, in spite of gossip which had at times linked Scott to what some thought were innovative and high-pressure schemes to raise his clients' incomes, I was not about to think ill of him. Together we could convince Dick that Fawcett was better for him.

The deal offered by the competitor was for ten books, each to feature Shell Scott, with payment of the million-dollar advance against royalty to be paced over a period of years for the author's tax advantage.

As Scott was consoling me over our possible loss of this valuable property, he further saddened me with his statement that, as Dick's agent, he could not permit him to take any less than he was being offered elsewhere.

Realizing this left no room for negotiating with the agent I asked Scott's permission to visit the author, my friend and his client, in his native California—a permission Scott graciously granted.

My first step was to have the accounting department make up an elaborate chart showing total print runs for each of the numerous printings of the many Shell Scott titles with earnings to-date and anticipated increased earnings from a larger royalty I was willing to give if he would stay. The total earnings anticipated more than one million dollars for the text ten books, but I was determined I would not match the million-dollar guarantee, which carried an unusual "no rejection" clause.

My chart and I flew to California where I joined forces at the Prather residence with an alerted and concerned Roscoe Fawcett, circulation director and by now a personal friend of both Prathers; also at hand was Fawcett's local circulation representative, Charles Rubessa, who had also become a personal friend of Mr. and Mrs. Prather.

All were cordial and I was complimented by Dick and Tina on the elaborate chart which both read with more interest than they might exhibit for any other printed material, except possibly one of Dick's own books. Drinks were poured in his elaborate bar, a delightful patio room open to the sky and around which the spacious, picturesque house was designed.

Meantime, Roscoe was bringing his very considerable persuasive talents to bear, in what seemed to promise good results for our mission.

"You guys sure do a great job," Prather enthused. "This chart is the most interesting thing I've ever seen. Can I keep it?"

"Sure," I murmured syruply, "and you can watch year by year to see how close we come to our estimate of sales and your earnings."

Then we went out to dinner, and Prather insisted on picking up the check for all five of us.

An author picking up a dinner check! I should have realized all was not serene.

Back at his house I elaborated on promotion plans for Dick's new book. He listened, but not raptly, and told us of a conviction borne out by astrology, numerology, or his own premonitions that his house, high on a mountain side, but a mile or so back from the shore, was going to fall into the sea. Earthquakes that would dump large areas of California into the Pacific had been prophesied by several local seers, and stories of such prognostications had appeared nationally in the media. Dick declared his conviction that the destruction was imminent. He stated he was going to sell his house and move, possibly to Hawaii or further inland in the United States. He was nervous and not happy over this threat.

No matter how we cajoled or pushed, he would not give us his decision of whether to stay with Fawcett that day. He wanted time to think everything over, and the agent would give us his decision later.

We left with a feeling that we had demonstrated that his best interests were served by us as his publishers. The last point we discussed before I returned to New York was one concerning a complaint he had about what he interpreted as a lack of appreciation for his work by the Fawcett editor assigned to him.

I told Dick that such a conclusion on his part was not warranted, but when I saw he was not convinced, I made my last concession. I told him I would be his editor and conduct all the correspondence concerning revisions, and so on. This I was willing to do because I always read each of his manuscripts anyway and had contributed many of the revision suggestions that had been incorporated in the letters written by the editor.

That, I thought, would be the clincher. After all, how many authors have a publisher for an editor!

The answer came quickly when I returned to New York. Prather would not move unless we matched the million-dollar guarantee on new books.

And that is how we lost the only author we have ever lost to a competitor in such a situation.

But the story doesn't end there. It developed that the new publisher with a million to spend was Pocket Books. Very soon it became known that the Shell Scott books published by his new publisher were not selling well, although we continued to reissue the earlier books in the series that we had contracts on with good sales.

There are many possible explanations for this seeming contradiction. I read several of Dick's new books and I could see what I thought was evidence that he was not getting the kind of editorial help he had received from us. The new covers and cover blurbs expressed none of the "fun and games" quality and identification that had made the Shell Scott series distinctive.

Several years later I visited Dick and Tina in their new palatial and even larger home perched on a hill outside of Phoenix, Arizona, in the exclusive Camelback section. Dick volunteered that changing publishers had "probably been a mistake." He spoke of moving his residence again. Arizona had not been lucky for him. He complained about the abundance of rattlesnakes on his grounds and demonstrated the gun he used regularly to blast the reptiles. He was particularly annoyed because the snakes sunned themselves on the edge of his swimming pool. The snakes, he ventured, were as troublesome as the earlier threat of an earthquake dropping his California home into the Pacific. He spoke vaguely about possibly taking a world cruise.

More recently I was approached by his agent again and was subtly allowed to infer that Dick might be able to disentangle himself from the million-dollar deal. Would Fawcett be interested in again working with the author? And if so, what would we guarantee as an advance?

My reply was that we could name no figure until we saw a finished manuscript, and that is the way the matter still stands.

Most publishers observe a rigorous code of conduct in the matter of publisher-author relations and would no more entertain the idea of singing a siren song of seduction to an author under contract to a brother publisher than they would think of setting fire to his offices.

It is not unknown for an author to switch publishers and usually for reasons both publisher and author may agree upon. It is entirely possible that you may elect to do so some day. If this happens it will not be without some of the kind of trauma that characterizes marital divorce, a trauma for both publisher and author but usually more destructive for the author.

A WRITER
IS A WRITER
IS A WRITER

It is possible you share an ill-considered idea, together with many other persons who have entertained the ambition of becoming writers, that the best road to writing success is to first work as a book editor.

Don't do it!

If you are employed as an editor now, and plan to be a writer, quit!

Drive a truck. Join the army. Invent a ten-layer hamburger sandwich. Get any job that will support you with the least drain on your physical and mental self and that will spare you time from working, sleeping, and eating in which to write.

It was not always so that a person spurred by a writing urge could afford to shape his life entirely to that end, but it is today.

The rewards for writing (particularly if your goal is so modest that you do not ascribe to quick ownership of a Manhattan town house, swimming pool, your own airplane, etc.) are easily demonstrated as equal to those of any profession. And the market for the writer's product is getting constantly larger and more rewarding.

In spite of my many-times-repeated advice to hordes of would-be writers applying for editorial jobs that writers gain nothing by working as editors, I have not convinced all of them that their writing ambition would be better served by simply writing and working outside the publishing industry.

Quite obviously this is true. It is as certain as the fact that a portrait painter would gain nothing by working in an art store as a picture framer.

Still, many cling to the conviction that if only they would work as an editor of books or magazines, somehow, possibly by osmosis, they would wake up some morning a writer.

Not so! Professional editing is a different craft entirely. An editor, if he is good, is the next most valuable person, second only to the author, in the quite sizable army of individuals, from typesetters to cover artists, who make their contributions to a book's success.

Each of these persons contributes his skill—and an editor's skill is not a writer's skill. The successful editor is an inspirer of authors: a relisher of the written word, an imaginative, warm person, capable of building deep, lasting friendships with the authors he works with. If he is to be truly tops in his craft, the editor must be by nature and inclination an entrepreneur: one whose burning, consuming ambition is to build and exploit a product of another—the author—for the profit of his publisher.

Editing is a worthwhile and wholly demanding career in itself; one that requires long hours, a high degree of professional skill and training, constant application, and all the acquired knowledge that can be accumulated for smoothing and facilitating harmonious relations between humans both inside and outside the office.

So constant is the stream of "I-want-to-be-a-writer" applicants for editorial jobs in book publishing and so deep-seated is this desire on the part of so many that I'm going to give a quick insight into just how a publishing house functions, so you may come to the conclusion, on your own, that to be a writer it is not desirable for you to first be an editor. Possibly, too, this information may cause you to switch your goal. Maybe you should be an editor, not a writer.

First, publishing house editorial staffs are not large. As few as five to ten editors in a medium-size house may be responsible for as many as one hundred books a year, or even more.

A beginner in the editorial business must settle for any available job, from secretary to mail-room employee to first reader. As many have demonstrated, the secretarial route is one most frequently and successfully used by editorial aspirants, both men and women. As secretary to several editors, an editor, or a publisher, you are in the position of knowing a lot about what is going on. You are very much "in the middle," where your viewpoint is not restricted to one special facet of the business, such as might be the case if you were a proofreader. It is a fact that more women become editors through this route than any other. There have always been male secretaries in publishing, some of them with a Ph.D., looking to become editors, and there seem to be even more recently.

When you have worked in a secretarial capacity and revealed intelligence, a willingness to work long hours, and a genuine love of words and books for a period of a year or more, you will be given preferential consideration for a beginning editorial job, particularly if you have been a voluntary, after-hours reader in the "slush pile" of unsolicited, submitted manuscripts. You will surely be tapped for promotion into editorial if you are lucky enough to rescue a publishable script from the slush. All publishers, I believe, would rather promote from within than fill beginners jobs with novices from other houses.

If you are good at spelling and have a keen eye for errors, you can qualify as a proofreader; this job has been known to lead to higher status, particularly copy-editing. But unless you are temperamentally suited, such a job is excruciatingly tedious. For anyone to do original writing of any value after sweating over the spelling, grammar, and syntax of another writer's work, as a copy editor or proofreader during the day, is impossible.

You might get a leg-in-the-door job toward being an editor in the publicity department if you have a background of newspaper work or secretarial work in some kind of publishing.

Once in a great while, if you have high scholastic accomplishments and your father is the publisher, you might start as a manuscript reader. This job of "reader" is almost a prerequisite to becoming a "producing editor," one who works with a stable of authors he has collected by plan and happenstance. The manuscript reader reads. He reads all day at his desk and frequently far into the night at home. He is cultivating a habit he will live with forever, should he prove able enough to move up to the exalted status of editor. Wherever he goes he will carry a briefcase, frequently two, loaded with manuscripts or proofs. He likes to read. He loves to read. He reads at night when others play bridge or watch TV. When he has no manuscripts or proofs to read, he reads books published by competitors and always the books on *The New York Times* list of bestsellers.

He reads on weekends when others play golf. And he loves it; but there is no energy, no time, no creative juice left in him for any writing up to the standards he might achieve if he were not so occupied with editorial responsibilities.

For all it would profit you as a writer to work in the editorial department of a publishing house, it would profit you more to work in the bookkeeping department where you could learn to keep accounts and records, a noticeable failure among authors. And working in accounting, or as a janitor, would give you a refreshing change of pace when you attacked the typewriter at night and on weekends.

Applicants for editorial jobs in book and magazine publishing are always surprised to find there are no writing jobs in the editorial department, only in the publicity or promotion department. In those departments wild, free-flowing, imaginative writing is encouraged and even rewarded so that glib puffery on book dust jackets or in publicity releases will enhance a book's sale.

So don't be an editor if you want to be a writer.

What, then, is the preparatory job that would best lead to professional authorship?

Newspaper reporting.

This answer is given so frequently it is a cliché, but true.

A vast number of successful authors of all kinds, from Ernest

Hemingway to Peg Bracken to Paul Gallico, have been reporters and newspaper writers. The authors with newspaper backgrounds total in the thousands. By writing for newspapers they learned the value of concise writing, accuracy, the basic elements in constructing a story, and the writing skills that will keep a reader reading. On the newspaper job they learned about people, about the reality of death and birth, about tragedy, revenge, jealousy, love, hate, and all the dark and joyous human experiences and emotions that are best seen firsthand to be written about with truth and distinction.

But newspaper reporting or writing can be a trap for someone who professes an ambition to write a novel or a book of some kind.

The fact is, a reporter gets such satisfaction from seeing his story in print, "on the front page no less," that his urge to write is too often satisfied for the moment. He promises himself and his admiring friends that he will write that book—someday. But he gets locked into his job. The writing he does every day pleases him: it is food enough for his ego, so that any hunger he may feel to create is fed by the writing he does for the newspaper, and the book he talked about writing is never written.

Of course, some reporters who dream about writing a book are simply too damn lazy.

The lazy ones are probably not very good reporters anyway and probably would not write a really worthwhile book.

Either reason for failure to write is a hell of a shame! Because every professional reporter, the Mr., Mrs. or Ms. who earns a living by writing and has done so for a period long enough to prove that he or she can write for newspaper publication, could write a book that would be bought by a book publisher—a novel or a nonfiction book.

Suppose you are a working reporter, or have been, and challenge my statement. What can I say that will persuade you that you *can* write such a book and sell it?

This whole book is intended to give that kind of persuasion and support, but something that might be more persuasive is this challenge:

Read one nonfiction book on the current best-seller list whose subject matter interests you.

Then ask yourself the questions: Could I, a reporter, have written that book?

Would readers enjoy my version? And answer these questions honestly.

Some of you I believe would be entitled to conclude, subjectively but honestly, that you could have done the job better. There isn't all that much magic involved in writing. After all, factual writing is an acquired skill: one that practice and application improves, and one in which many persons could demonstrate proficiency superior to that found in many published books.

If you write a nonfiction book you must have either firsthand knowledge of the subject or work as a collaborator with some expert who does have such firsthand knowledge. You must write on something about which you are informed; reporters do this constantly. Probably, too, you should write about something in which you have an interest, old or newly acquired; something you can write about with compelling enthusiasm.

The following are examples of such books, each a bestseller.

How To Build And Contract Your Own Home by Larry Eisinger is a book written and illustrated by someone who planned, supervised, and helped build his own home, complete with swimming pool and sauna bath. This is an original paperback, and Fawcett sold more than 500,000 copies at a high cover price.

Another nonfiction book that has sold many millions is *The Amazing Results of Positive Thinking* by Norman Vincent Peale, a book adapted from the author's sermons, as are many of his books—all of them best-sellers.

Others include such divergent subjects as *How to Make ESP Work for You* by Harold Sherman, and a book that became the No. 1 best-seller, *The Bermuda Triangle* by Charles Berlitz with J. Manson Valentine. This last book was a cleverly related account of ships, planes, and people lost mysteriously in an area of the Atlantic Ocean between Florida and Bermuda, a strange but well-known phenomenon that many editors or writers might think had been written to death in newspaper features and magazine stories. But the opposite is frequently true. Readers like the familiar. Frequently they prefer to have a smattering of knowledge or information on the subjects they read about in books; it seems just enough information of a provocative nature had appeared in print to guarantee success for these authors who gathered up all the facts and threw in some enticing rumors and imaginative theories as to what might explain the mysterious tragedies.

Enough in that direction. It is not my intention to tell you how to write a book or what to write about. Rather, I want to whip up your desire and spur your ambition until you write the book of your choice in your own way. Along that line I'm going to tell you about a newspaper writer and reporter who was forced by a big mouth, his own, to write a book.

The writer is Bruce Catton, now world-famous as a Pulitzer Prize-winning author of popular Civil War histories, whose books are written with the vivid storytelling skill of a novelist.

Bruce is the "David Niven" type: thin, handsome, and possessed with a casual and nearly constant smile that manages to be both sardonic and warm.

Before I met him I had frequently admired his choice of female luncheon companions, with whom I would see him lifting a very dry martini in the Oak Room of the Algonquin Hotel. These girls always seemed to radiate both physical beauty and intelligence. There was nothing flashy about them—each was a perfect complement in dress and manner to the carefully tailored Mr. Catton, who was usually attired in a modest pinstripe or charcoal gray suit with a tie of regimental stripe. Conversation between Mr. Catton and his attractive companions was always animated. Clearly he liked these girls, and they liked him.

There came a day when Bruce was lunching alone and, since I've always been an author-worshipper, I suggested to Raul the headwaiter that he introduce me to Mr. Catton, which he did. After ascertaining that Mr. Catton was alone, I asked him to join me and my guest, but all three of us ended up at his table. There I pried out of him the story of his first book success.

His had been a wide and varied newspaper experience. He had been a reporter on the Boston *Herald American* and a reporter and rewrite man on the Cleveland *News Sun* and the Cleveland *Plain Dealer* prior to his joining the Scripps Howard syndicate, and moving to Washington, D.C.

Bruce gained a legendary reputation in Cleveland as a star rewrite man, I found out subsequently. For those who don't know, the rewrite man on a large daily paper is to the rest of the staff as the aerialist is to the other performers in a circus.

He is the aristocrat. He is the star performer who, with cigarette dangling and vest open, sits at his typewriter and types at lightning speed into clear, coherent form, the story coming to him through telephonic headphones in a bare recital of basic facts from the reporter at the scene of the crash, fire, or murder. His is the job-most-aspired-to in the city room. He is the one watched with wild-eyed amazement by cub reporters as his thundering typewriter spews out a running ribbon of paper, frequently ripped off in short takes by the copy editor with no slackening of the pounding keys, so that the pieces of copy may be edited speedily and rushed in separate paragraphs to be cast into metal type even as the story continues to be written.

That's the way it is in the movies and in real life too.

Bruce's stories were much admired as masterful newspaper writing and reporting, and the question his co-workers were constantly asking him with interest, awe, and respect was, "When are you going to write that novel?"

"Frankly, I always thought I would write a novel sometime," Bruce confessed to me, "and the constant repetition of the question forced me to give an answer. Until I was about thirty-five, I would answer simply, 'Someday.'

"When I passed age thirty-five, I began to answer the question with, 'Before I'm fifty.' "

Then one morning Bruce awakened to the realization that he had reached his forty-ninth birthday. He had not written the novel he had so many times told people he would write before he was fifty, or even started to write it, or thought much about what he might write.

That was the morning he decided to devote full time to book writing. "I'm going to write a novel," he said. "I'll give six months to the project."

He wrote and rewrote, literally day and night, pushing himself to the goal he had set.

At the end of three months he was halfway through a novel of the Old South and he sat down to read what he had written.

"It had been the hardest labor I ever performed," Bruce said. "The writing of all those words . . . and the manuscript reflected just that—labor.

"When I finished reading what I had written, I threw the whole thing in the wastebasket.

"What I had done, I realized, was to force myself to write a very bad imitation of *Gone with the Wind*, Margaret Mitchell's big best-seller of the day. My manuscript was so dreadful, my fear was that someone might read it as something I had written. So I burned it; an experience that marked what was surely the lowest moment of my life.

"What to do? In 1949 I had written a factual book about the men who headed up the war effort, called *War Lords of Washington*. It had been published to bad reviews and bad sales. Another book like that would not satisfy my need to write a book people would read, admire, and react warmly to—a story!

"In writing my ill-starred effort at a novel, I had chosen a background of the Civil War—a period about which I was well informed. Even though I was convinced my novel was hopeless, I was still interested in the War Between the States. Indeed, the Civil War had been my longtime hobby interest, so I continued at my typewriter writing a book of nonfiction about the Army of the Potomac. In a few months I had finished the book and I liked it."

It would be pleasant to bring this story to a smash ending by reporting that Bruce sold this manuscript on first submission for that favorite figure, one million dollars, but such was not the case.

51

Harcourt Brace, to whom he submitted the book, turned it down on the grounds that it was impossible to sell Civil War books.

"I knew an editor in another publishing house, and he seemed quite enthusiastic, so I sent the manuscript to him," Bruce related. "His house also rejected it for the same reason the first one had.

"By this time I was feeling somewhat desperate. I knew no other publisher and did not care for the idea of sending the manuscript around blind. Eventually, I consulted George Braziller, who had the Book Find Club, a man I knew slightly. George read the manuscript and said that while it was nothing the Book Find Club could handle, he would see if he could find a publisher. He succeeded—may heaven bless him—and in the course of time Doubleday brought out *Mr. Lincoln's Army* in 1951."

Bruce went on to write his great series of highly acclaimed books of the Civil War. In 1952 he brought out *Glory Road* and in 1953, *A Stillness At Appomattox*, which won the Pulitzer Prize for History. He has never gone back to newspapering.

HOUSEWIVES, DOCTORS, LAWYERS, TEACHERS AS AUTHORS

The only occupation that may have produced more authors of novels than newspapering is, I believe, that of housewife. This is obviously because it has been the historic lot of women to be tied to their houses by cooking, sewing, and raising children. Thus encumbered, a housewife can, if she's determined, slip in a few hours or minutes a day with pen, pencil, or typewriter while the kids are in bed, in school, or out in the yard.

I have known cases where those "few hours or minutes" were after the rest of the household was in bed, and sometimes the hours lasted until dawn. Surely a woman with a creative urge to write chafes under the tedium of housework, and it may be the very restless distaste she feels for such chores that drives her to the release she gets in writing. And many, many of these women have gone on to careers as novelists and writers. Taylor Caldwell, author of a succession of more than twenty brilliant successes starting with *Dynasty of Death*, is one; Mary Stewart, who has written many popular suspense novels and more recently the much acclaimed serious but popular novel *The Crystal Cave*, is another. Helen MacInnes, whose every novel makes the best-seller list, is among those who at one time was or still is a housewife, as was Dorothy Eden,

Norah Lofts, Phyllis Whitney, Victoria Holt, Jane Aiken Hodge, and almost all of the other women writers whose works have been published.

Two others must be mentioned: Margaret Mitchell, housewife, whose one book *Gone with the Wind* reposed in her trunk unsubmitted until a friend told a publisher's employee of its whereabouts, is one. The other is Grace Metalious, wife of an embattled high school teacher, who decided to put a rather inflammatory, fictionalized version of her community and her husband's school into a novel, *Peyton Place.* Both of these novels are among the top five in sales of all novels in the English language. It was *Peyton Place* that set a record for rejections of a book destined for best-seller status; it was turned down by more than a dozen publishers. Finally a reader, Ms. Leona Nevler, now publisher of Fawcett paperbacks, persuaded Kitty Messner, head of Julian Messner Inc., to publish the Metalious novel.

Way back on one of these meandering pages, I referred to "happenstance," as having been so often the unplanned event that turned someone into a published author. Certainly of all the odd "happenstances" that led to writing and successful authorship, Jessamyn West's is the most unusual I have ever encountered.

In reply to my seeking verification of the anecdote and a request for any encouraging suggestions she might have for would-be writers, the author of *The Friendly Persuasion, The Massacre at Fall Creek,* and other best-sellers sent the following in a letter: "After two bedfast years with tuberculosis, a friend suggested to me that I 'piece a quilt,' so that I could leave my mother something to remember me by.

"Instead of making a quilt I decided that if my case were that desperate, I'd do what I'd always wanted to do—write a book.

"But you know that nothing as complex as writing a book comes about in quite so simple and clean a fashion.

"I had always wanted to write and was always afraid that to do so was presumptuous, egotistical. My background was rural and Quaker. There one is taught, don't stick your neck out; don't take a chance; don't give yourself away; don't make a fool of yourself. And of course to be a writer all those risks must be taken, as you know.

"So, afraid to write, but wanting to keep close to writing, I had worked for my Ph.D. in English at the University of California, at Berkeley. The date was set for my doctor's orals, then it was postponed a week because one of the professors was ill. During that week I had a hemorrhage, and three days later I was in a sanatorium with far-advanced tuberculosis.

"It was ten years before I began to lead a semi-normal life.

53

"When I had to give up my work for my doctorate, I thought my life had ended; and doctors thought it was ended, period. I sometimes think that as a would-be writer I chose to have a disease that would make my career as a professor (that's what I had in mind) impossible, and my life as a writer possible. In other words, I painted myself into a corner where there was just room for me and a pen.

"I was helped in my decision to try to write by Maureen Hayes (Mrs. Mike Mansfield) who had been a fellow student at California. She sent me copies of the old *Frontier* and *Midland* magazines, and in them I saw stories of the kind I thought I might write: stories less mechanically plotted than those in popular magazines.

"I do not outline a complete novel, either in my mind or on paper before I start writing.

"A novel that doesn't grow, the characters who do not develop, change, interact in ways unforseen by me would be as boring for me to write as a novel completely foreseen at the beginning by the reader would be boring for him to read. I am a writer, writing, not a typist putting on to paper the description of a series of scenes that have moved across my mind's film.

"I like to work in the morning. I haven't an office or secretary and am subject to the interruptions any housewife endures. It is impossible to convince friends and relatives that writing demands as much attention and consideration from others as would be accorded the checkout girl at the Safeway. So, I work in the morning and into the afternoon, using what time I am permitted and what energy I have."

And that is how Jessamyn West did it and continues to do it.

Many doctors have been successful novelists. Richard Llewellyn of *How Green Was My Valley* fame comes quickly to mind. Many have written movingly and successfully of their professional experiences. One of these, William A. Nolen, M.D., has written five books in almost as many years, while responsibly performing the demanding tasks of chief of surgery. His first book was *The Making of a Surgeon*, his next, *A Surgeon's World*, and his third, *Healing: A Doctor in Search of a Miracle*. In the list of doctor-authors we must include Sir Arthur Conan Doyle, a rather unsuccessful physician who became the famous creator of Sherlock Holmes.

Lawyers have proved to be good and interesting writers, and I would argue that any trial lawyer who can move a jury can also write books that will move readers. Louis Nizer has written at least three best-sellers, including *My Life in Court* and *The Implosion Conspiracy*.

Louis Auchincloss, an active lawyer, has somehow found time

to write two dozen delightful and popular novels, most of them entertainingly, interpreting the legal profession, as does his most recent *The Partners*. The list of lawyer-authors is long.

Even veterinarians write international best-sellers, as witness *All Things Bright and Beautiful* by Yorkshireman James Herriot.

I believe the biggest relatively untapped reservoir of potential best-selling authors is the teaching profession and those who live in university campus communities.

Since I attended three colleges—graduating from one and kicked out of one—and filled some speaking engagements at others, I feel in a position to state with authority that no area on our globe holds and nurtures as many candidates for successful authorship as do the campus communities. I include in these communities those persons who may have no official connection with a university but are seemingly attracted to it and become a part of it by engaging in its activities or moving socially with its residents.

Among those Fawcett authors who left teaching to become professional—and wealthy—writers are James A. Michener, Isaac Asimov, Dorothy Eden, and Shirley Ann Grau. Among those who have attained fame as writers and still, by some miracle of "time compression," teach a full course load is Joyce Carol Oates.

I won't limit the high potential of authorship to college teachers. Many high school and grade school teachers are real or potential authors.

It follows then that anyone who acquires knowledge, as a teacher does, and makes a profession of imparting knowledge and ideas to others in the classroom could do the same kind of job on the pages of a book—either a novel, or a nonfiction book, possibly a textbook.

It is accepted and expected that university teachers will write textbooks, and some of these have proven gigantic earners for the author.

It seems that fewer teachers write novels than texts or factual books. This may be so because teachers are in awe of the novel, or are too timid and too inhibited by conformity to express themselves in the novel form. Certainly many teachers have a great personal interest in novels, read them devotedly, and have an intelligent sensitivity that is natural to novelists. Also, many of them have a specialty—knowledge which they might interpret in the novel form.

Many teachers have confessed to me that they feel the desire to create—to write a novel or a popular book. Some have stifled this urge as unseemly and not suited to their image as a pedagogue. Some have refused to make the creative effort from cowardice—afraid to fail. Yes, I'm sure every university campus group includes some of that kind of coward. These are the persons who have acquired a stature of culture and ego-pleasing superiority of one kind or another. They have reached a sort of halfway retirement from competitive living, an escape from the harsher realities of life, and are afraid to court possible rejection of a book or novel.

Some of these able persons are just plain lazy, too. They use the same "put-off" as do reporters, as did Bruce Catton. "I'll write a book," they tell themselves and sometimes friends and family, but they lack the guts, determination, and energy exhibited by the author of *A Stillness At Appomatox*. When they get to age forty-nine, as did Catton, they don't say, "I'll do it before I'm fifty." Instead they are content to say, "It's too late now. I'm too old."

You are never "too old." One dramatic instance of this concerns a first novel written by a man when he was over seventy, a much imitated book and one that has sold millions of copies. The book is *Mandingo* by Kyle Onstott. Kyle was a most cultured individual, an authority on dogs, and an internationally famous judge of them at exhibitions and shows. His novel, which reflected life on pre-Civil War slave-breeding plantations, sprang out of his interest and collection of old plantation journals and account books that he gathered when he was a visiting judge at plantations in our South and in South America and the Caribbean.

Perhaps nowhere is there such an exaggerated, stultifying reverence for the novel and authorship as among teachers. It would seem all too many of them, through a long, old-fashioned, formal education, have been victims of literature courses which stressed to absurdity the divinity of the classics. Instead of accepting these sometimes beautiful, sometimes dreary, sometimes imagination-stirring works as products of man, with an option to reject those that do not appeal, they were often taught that all the classics, and those who wrote them, must be accorded the infallibility of Holy Writ and the deities.

This sad state seems to have caused great guilt among some who were force-fed the classics. They admit only to themselves that much that was stuffed down their gullets as mind- and soul-stirring was for them, dull and confusing.

Don't let failure to appreciate everything that has been written prevent you from writing what you want to write. Sound off about what you don't like and fight in defense of what you do like. Such emotion-stirring antics are not only a healthy cathartic, but lead to creative expression, and that is just another name for writing.

If you feel a stirring within you, a desire to write something that will genuinely please yourself and others, do so. The effort will bring you happiness, and the result may bring you more tangible rewards.

If you are beginning to get the idea that I am most concerned and strongly convinced there is a great waste of writing talent among teachers and others in our educational communities, you are right.

While I am concerned with the fact that the publishing industry does not have enough good manuscripts to publish, my adrenaline flows even more for the reason that the teachers, the graduate students, and others on the campus could be getting a satisfaction they never dreamed of by producing books people want to read!

A TALE ABOUT ERNEST HEMINGWAY

Sometimes what starts out as a short story won't work as such, but turns into a novel, or as happened in at least one instance, becomes both a short story and a very famous novel. I happened to be a participant in such a noteworthy circumstance—one that took a most dramatic turn and has considerable human interest because it concerned The Great One, Ernest Hemingway.

This happened when Papa lived in Cuba, and my job was editorial director of Fawcett and publisher of our then recently started paperback division. *True*, the man's magazine then published by Fawcett, was doing very well, and since I invented the magazine I took an active part in its editing and was proud of having the largest circulation ever attained by a man's magazine, something over two million monthly. Much of our circulation success was ascribed to stories written by "name" authors and I was determined to get the king of them all, Papa, Big He of the Caribbean, the most manly writer of them all. So I suggested to the editor of *True*, Mr. Ken Purdy, that he approach The Great One to write for us.

In 1950 Ken was successful in getting Hemingway to write a short, nonblood-stirring piece about his experiences hunting pronghorn antelope in Idaho. We paid him $3,700 for this piece and urged him to do more and quickly. Correspondence was not very satisfactory because our urgings had to be sent to Hemingway's lawyer-agent who had helped us obtain the first piece.

Then one afternoon in November or December of 1950, Ken Purdy came charging into my office with the news that Hemingway was in New York and had agreed to meet with us and discuss new projects the following morning at eleven. "Bring him up to my office," I said. "Let's get something really worthwhile out of him."

The Great One showed up about forty-five minutes late by himself. Conversation was loose and enjoyable. Hemingway indicated that he was willing to write for *True* on a regular basis, but he wanted what he defined as "Big Money."

"What kind of story do you want from me?" he asked after I assured him I thought we could get together on Big Money.

The gist of what I suggested was: "Write a true experience story about a sport you like most. Write it in such a way that it will stir the emotions and excite the reader—permit him to live the experience you are writing about. We want a *story* not an article."

"That would have to be a big piece," he mused, "longer than the usual magazine article."

"How long?" I asked.

He reflected a moment and replied, "I could write what I have in mind in about ten thousand words."

"What is the subject?" I inquired.

"Fishing for blue marlin," he replied. "A great true story. How much will you pay me?"

"We'll pay you a dollar a word," I answered. "Ten thousand dollars for ten thousand words."

Obviously he was surprised and pleased at the price, which was something of a record in those long gone days. We shook hands on the deal and he went off to Cuba, promising the manuscript in a month or so. "I'll have more stories for you, too," he said.

Several weeks passed and Ken Purdy came into my office with the news that Hemingway's agent reported there was something wrong. Papa had a question. The story was underway but not finished. It was suggested we call Papa on the phone.

His voice came over loud and clear. "The story is bigger than I thought," he explained. "I have now written nearly fifteen thousand words and the story is no more than half finished. How much will you pay me for this bigger story?"

This was a puzzler, as there was no way we could accommodate a story of possibly thirty thousand words in the pages of one issue, and we had a policy of no serials or continued stories.

"Send it along when it's finished," I urged. "We'll make you an offer when we see how much of it we can publish."

"It would be impossible to cut this story," he replied, an edge in his tone that implied I was suggesting a knife to his jugular. "You agreed to pay ten thousand dollars for a ten-thousand-word story. It would seem a larger story would still be worth a dollar a word."

I wasn't about to tell him I had strained the budget with the ten thousand dollar price, and I was not going to commit us to an undefined number of words at a dollar per word. Again I urged him to send the manuscript for our inspection when he was finished so we might make a new offer.

I shall never forget his final words as he rather irately rejected my suggestion.

"I shall finish the story," he said in clipped tones, "and put it in my trunk. It will be better there than money in the bank!"

We got no more stories from Ernest. But on September 1, 1952, *Life* magazine published a thirty-thousand-word "novel" by Ernest Hemingway in one issue entitled *The Old Man and the Sea*.

Could this be our story of blue marlin fishing? It concerned blue marlin, alright, but the adventure was that of an old Cuban fisherman, and we had rather expected a personal adventure of the author's.

The Old Man and the Sea was published by Scribner's in hardcover a week or so after publication in *Life*, was a popular choice of the Book-of-the-Month Club, and attracted worldwide attention and very favorable reviews. It is Hemingway's biggest-selling novel, won the Pulitzer Prize for Literature, and contributed hugely to his being awarded the Nobel Prize.

Even after publication of the book, I had only a vague thought that the story Hemingway had agreed to write for our magazine might in some way be connected with the story in *Life* and published to such fame as a novel.

Could it possibly be the same story? I wondered. But Hemingway called this book a novel, and the story he agreed to write for us was not a work of fiction. He represented it to us as a true story.

Then some time after the book won worldwide acclaim, a New York newspaper published an interview with a tiny, wizened old Cuban fisherman, who was quoted as insisting that *The Old Man and the Sea* was in every respect a true story—the true story of his experience with a giant blue marlin.

The final answer did not come until after a physically and mentally shattered, but proudly disciplined Hemingway orchestrated his own dramatic death. Then it was he selected a shotgun in his Idaho home early one sunny morning while his wife slept upstairs, loaded both barrels of the tight-choked twelve-gauge gun, and set the triggers for firing.

Next in orderly fashion, he put the butt of the gun on the floor, leaned his forehead against the open ends of both barrels and, in what must have been a victor's smile, speeded the so apparent disir..egration of body and mind from disease by flicking off both triggers.

The top of the old warrior's head was blown off abc ve the eyes, appropriately, by a silver-inlaid field gun—a Boss—accepted as one of the finest in the world. "Well done. Clean kill," I think Hemingway would have said.

Never one to give up, and after an interval I hoped would be considered acceptable, I wrote his widow, Mary. "Is it possible," I inquired, "that the marlin story Mr. Hemingway was writing for us in 1950 was finished and is still in his trunk."

I told her of her late husband's comment, "It will be better there than money in the bank."

Back came her letter in reply: "*The Old Man and the Sea* is the only story Ernest ever wrote about blue marlin fishing."

Then in 1969 with publication of the carefully detailed biography, *Ernest Hemingway: A Life Story* by Carlos Baker, I learned more about the origin and history of the Cuban fisherman's story.

The Old Man and the Sea, Carlos Baker reports, was indeed a true story. The adventure of an old Cuban fisherman, one Senor Santiago, was told to Hemingway in 1935 by Carlos Gutierrez. The author made immediate use of it in a short story, "On the Blue Water," published in the April 1936 *Esquire*.

In a letter Hemingway wrote in 1939 there is evidence he intended to write the story again in greater detail.

Even after he had finished the final version in 1951 it would seem he did not consider it a novel in the real sense, but one story of a several-section book he planned to write about the sea, the first long section of which he had nearly completed. Originally this book was to have three sections. Then the plan changed and he decided to make the story of the old fisherman the fourth and last section of the long book. It was called at this point, "The Santiago Story," after the name of the old man in the story.

There can, under all the circumstances, be little doubt that the feature story he started to write for *True* became the novel he finished in 1951. He showed the manuscript proudly to many of his friends but made no effort to have it published as a book, alone, until after Leland Hayward read it in manuscript and suggested submitting it to *Life* magazine for publication in a single issue. Only a few weeks earlier Hemingway had shown a typed script to Jack O'Connell, editor of *Cosmopolitan* magazine. O'Connell was enthusiastic about the story and wanted to publish it in a single issue of *Cosmopolitan*. The deal fell through when all O'Connell offered was ten thousand dollars.

In addition to pointing up the fact that an author's idea and his manuscript may end up in a medium other than the one originally intended or, indeed, in two mediums, there is another aspect of authorship that is important and worth commenting on here.

And that is, this factual story is a novel because Hemingway, the author, says it is; despite the fact that my dictionary says a novel is a fictitious prose narrative of a considerable length.

I have, I believe, read every book written by Hemingway, and many books about him, and I understand thoroughly that he made his own rules and definitions. I'm strongly inclined to the idea too that his belief in himself, in his own eminence, was so great that he did not distinguish between fact and fiction in his own writing. If he wrote a piece of "considerable" length it earned the distinction of being called "novel," because Ernest Hemingway had contributed the artistry and skill that made the facts of the old man's fishing adventure more than a true story or a book of nonfiction. It had become his work of art. Not one word must be changed. If there is something about it you do not like, that is your fault—an imperfection in your reading taste buds.

He had started a long factual story for a magazine called *True*, which he knew did not publish fiction, and he had finished it as his artistry dictated. It did not appear in *True* because we would not guarantee a dollar a word at the longer, unknown length. *Life* paid him forty thousand dollars for about twenty-five thousand words. If *True* had published *The Old Man and the Sea* it would not have been called a novel by us. Probably by him.

Certainly the author is entitled to his definition of his work. I subscribe to the idea, too, that the author is entitled to whatever degree of outrageous belief in his work will keep him reasonable, sanguine, and producing.

Perhaps this is the place to comment on author ego, so soon after mentioning Hemingway—popularly believed and agreed to have an ego second in size only to Mt. Kilimanjaro and more abrasive than a coral atoll.

I happen to be of the conviction that an author's ego is somehow tied to the seat of his creativity, and that without a prominent and vigorous ego there can be no big or superior writing. To excise the ego unduly is to castrate the author.

If you can sit placidly, perhaps gratefully, while another slashes your copy with an editing pencil, removing words, changing sentences, and feel no deep urge to plunge the despoiler's pencil into his thorax, there is a good chance you will never be an author.

There is sound reason for this. The author is the creator. It is he

61

who gives birth to characters and situations—moves the people of his story with a fluid ease to the earth's farthest corners or into stellar space.

The author is God. To alter his will or change his words is an affront to a deity. Like Jehovah, the author is a god of wrath. If someone despoils his creation, he is entitled to a Jehovian howl.

Seriously, unless you get at least a bit red-necked at another's criticism of your writing, even though later in private you may agree with him, there is little hope for you as a creative writer.

There is sometimes an intelligent, fortunate middle ground in a harmonious author-editor relationship, with such understanding on each side, that the editor can say to the author of an offending paragraph, "This stinks, pal."

Once, he can say it. Twice, at his own risk.

Actually I have seen a few instances in which older, very experienced authors have mellowed to a degree that they can take a critical suggestion without getting pop-eyed and yelling foul obscenities.

They are not fooling me, though. As they nod agreeably and consent to a minor change, they have (and I know it) retired into a Walter Mitty dreamworld. There they are even now running white-hot spears through my most tender parts, and their smiles are not of acquiescence to the change requested but diabolical leers as my blood pours out on the office floor.

Our educational process exerts a constant pressure to destroy the individual ego, to force all personalities into a predictable norm. We are taught that it is unforgiveably selfish to have that certain dominant belief in oneself that may be an absolute and necessary part of the practical, creative process in man.

I do wonder, in that connection, if one reason so many of those intelligent, delightful people on campus don't write more novels and books is that they have been shaped into people who are too polite, too considerate of the other guy's opinion, incapable of being sure of themselves as an author must be—even, sometimes, when he's wrong.

IT'S A DO-IT-YOURSELF BUSINESS

Back a few pages I heard a number of readers gasp in puzzled disbelief when I said at least a third of America's book publishers do not read unsolicited manuscripts but return them to authors unopened.

I'll give you a further hint that becoming a successful author is not easy by repeating what I once said rather spiritedly to fellow directors of the Association of American Publishers: "The publishing industry does not do a God-damned thing to encourage authors."

Maybe some day someone will devise a way in which all publishers can join in a calculated plan to encourage and develop authors as the lumber industry plants and cultivates tree seedlings under government control, but I doubt it.

The book publishing industry as a whole is unable to give authors anything but a competitive chance to find a publisher among its members. There is no source of revenue for the industry, or its association, to make meaningful contributions to training authors or sustaining them on any sort of writers' welfare-relief. Neither can the oil industry spend funds drilling cooperatively to find oil wells to be shared by Exxon, Gulf, and Texaco. Drill your own well is the rule, and so it is in publishing. Find your own writer and tie him up with contracts.

Individual publishers make efforts of differing degrees to find and develop new authors, or rather, their editors do. A top-notch editor always has his antenna out and quivering in anticipation of finding someone with a book idea and the ability to write it. Newspaper features, magazine articles, scientific and medical journals are read eagerly by book editors for leads to book ideas or new writers to write books. Some editors make a habit of attending conventions of the Western Writer's Association or the regular meetings of the Mystery Writers, and some have found it profitable to visit college campuses and seek out those who might be capable and willing to write a book.

A few editors do contribute modestly with their presence at "writer conference" activities, but I detect less than enthusiasm for such gatherings among the publishers. The track record for successful authors seems to point more clearly to the writer who just keeps on writing until he sells his book, than to the writers who attend such talk fests.

Neither does the college or university "writer-in-residence" syndrome get much serious attention from publishers, although a few books and novels have resulted from such altruistic programs. Now and then an editor will give a talk at such a think tank, but usually only if the writer-in-residence is the editor's protégé and makes urgent demands. I suppose any intelligent effort to encourage authorship should be endorsed, but many editors are skeptical of a situation in which one writer is telling another writer how to write, or "helping" him in any way, particularly if the writer-in-residence may be of callow years and small professional success, but equipped with the usual standard author equipment, the big "I." Perhaps such conclaves are worth observing for the education would-be novelists receive: what happens when people of opposite sexes are in close sweaty proximity busily probing each others' minds. Some stories I've heard make these in-residence digs sound more swinging than a singles' bar.

I admit a prejudice against such efforts that I know about, on how to teach novel-writing in colleges. Yet my instinct is to applaud anyone who makes an effort to help authors, and certainly the writer-in-residence scheme is well-meaning.

I'm inclined to look at the backgrounds of yesterday's and today's successful writers and say, "See, they made it on their own, with hard work, spirit, and dedication. And they did it their own way."

My hunch is that "their own way" may be more important in building a truly successful author than is generally known. Possibly it is by his exposure to his personal turmoil and strife—meeting and solving problems by himself—that the author develops the vague yet distinct tracings of his person that reflect in his writings, that separate him by style, manner, and traits from all other writers. It is this unique glimmer and sheen that readers react to.

Indeed, if writing were only mechanical we could have novel schools as they have journalism schools, where all are taught to write news stories alike. "Write leads alike," they teach. "Write short sentences and tell who, what, where, when, and how."

If there is a true artistry in writing, it is that of personalized expression, and I would be suspicious that writers-in-residence efforts may inhibit the individual's expression.

Bennett Cerf used to make what he called "the college circuit," a series of speeches at about a dozen colleges, three times a year. Bennett's friends kidded him that he made these trips to laugh at his own jokes and hear himself talk, but I think he was serious in his efforts to be of assistance to authors and find writers for Random House.

When asked if he found any new writers on his trips, Bennett rattled off quite a list of names, but I only remember one—Rod McKuen—and Bennett's "finding" him was related thus by Bennett: "I was talking in the afternoon in the auditorium of some Western college, perhaps San Jose State," Bennett said. "I was answering questions after finishing my talk and there was the usual crowd of kids gathered around. One older-looking fellow waited until the others left before introducing himself as Rod McKuen, with the information that he was 'a visiting artist,' scheduled to sing some of his own songs to his own guitar accompaniment that night. He was on tour and inquired if we at Random House might be interested in publishing some of his poetry.

"I passed on the bad news—what everyone in publishing knows—that you can't publish poetry profitably.

"He was very polite and commented sadly that he guessed he had been pretty lucky to sell nearly forty thousand copies of his self-published book of poetry.

" 'How many copies?' I sputtered.

" 'Forty thousand,' he repeated, 'and I'm going to have to order more from my printer. I'm sold out.' "

That information on McKuen's popularity and salability was enough for Bennett to sign him up quickly, poetry or no poetry, and Random sold hundreds of thousands of each of Rod McKuen's books of poetry that followed.

After several years and many McKuen best-sellers, Random felt they had to grant McKuen's unusual demand to be a co-publisher of his own books, probably as a tax-saving gimmick. So demanding did he become that eventually Random gave McKuen up, and he went to another publisher.

Rod McKuen's having first published his own book successfully may have given some of you the idea that you can publish your manuscripts yourself.

Don't do it. His is a most unusual success, due in great part to thousands of personal appearances of that melancholic, handsome, dissipated profile and the singing of his verses to his own guitar accompaniment. The thousands he sold of his own edition were sold from the platform after his performances. He continues to promote his own literary wares in colleges and major cities throughout the world. The announcement of McKuen in Concert sells out Carnegie Hall and, apparently, he plays everywhere to full houses. These enthusiastic fans buy his verse in bookstores everywhere.

Possibly the only kind of book subject that might justify self-publishing is a local subject, one that would not be properly served by a national publisher; such as a local guide book, a local photo collection, or a cookbook put together by the Ladies' Aid Society.

Do not fall for the "vanity publisher" ads you see in some newspapers and magazines. To the uninitiated the offer to "print, distribute, and sell your book," at your expense, has all the attraction of Kewpie doll games at a carnival for a country bumpkin, and just as much validity.

Now back to that statement several times stated that my telephone-conducted poll indicates some publishers return unsolicited manuscripts unopened and unread to unpublished authors.

It is a fact.

Since this is true, how then can an unknown author get his first book published?

There are ways.

Before I reveal the secret routes to the editor's scrutiny, let me tell you why some publishers, but not all, have reached the conclusion that the slush pile of unsolicited manuscripts is not worth straining for publishable lumps.

This refuse-to-read judgment is made for economic reasons, based on the personal experiences of many publishers. They have found that so few of the submitted manuscripts by unpublished authors are recognized as publishable, that to have them evaluated by competent editors simply costs too much. Even those publishers who read the slush admit that to do so is impractical from a cost standpoint.

The bigger publishers admit to receiving more than ten thousand book manuscript submissions each, by unknown authors annually. You can take heart that well over ninety-five percent of these submissions are patently hopeless at a glance, and thus may let your submitted jewel shine brightly against a background of dross. And it has happened many, many times, that a diligent editor has found a publishable manuscript in the slush pile.

The one tragedy of the slush pile, among many, is that an editor's sensibilities are so blunted after hours of reading page after page of hopeless, limping prose that he is unlikely to recognize signs of value in the occasional worthy manuscript.

The very volume of these submissions discourages an editor who may already have more projects on hand with known authors than he can meet the deadlines on.

Too frequently the first inspection of the slush pile is left to the ambitious mail-room boy or steno to decide which manuscript can be sent back pronto with a rejection slip and which to send along for an editor's appraisal.

In some publishing houses the slush is allowed to accumulate for weeks or months, until it is a veritable mountain of manuscripts.

For an editor to gnaw away at such a physically threatening pile is to give him another excuse for the second and third martini at lunch.

One fact that will give authors the encouragement they crave and are entitled to is that any book editor gives a squeal of delight when he recognizes the name of a published writer on a submitted manuscript. He opens that manuscript envelope with all the urgency of a child unwrapping a Christmas package.

Don't take that as an invitation to substitute the name of a famous author of a best-seller on the return address of your manuscript envelope, although it might work at that. Rather, accept the circumstances as indicating that the editor does want to find a publishable manuscript each time he casts his eye on the first page of any submitted work.

Certainly your manuscript will get complete attention and eager reading if your accompanying letter reveals you have had something published in magazines, newspapers, or elsewhere.

However, there are ways to get your manuscript read, even though you have not written for publication.

My telephone poll does reveal some encouraging facts. More companies are reading the slush than before; a reflection I'm sure of the manuscript shortage. One publisher reports he is contemplating payment of a five hundred dollar bonus to editor or reader for each publishable manuscript rescued from the slush, one that can be published as is or after therapeutic resuscitation by editor and author.

I would like to be of service to you by listing the names of those publishers who return book manuscripts unread, but this would not be helpful or fair, considering that publishers are capable of changing their habits.

So, instead of using this sorry information as an excuse for not writing that book, accept it as a competitive condition that exists, in one form or another, throughout the creative world. Even a race horse must "break its maiden," before it can run in a featured race; and a lawyer must win at least one case in court before his services are eagerly sought out. He may struggle for years to get that first case or the one that leads to success.

Now that you are aware of this first hurdle: your submitted manuscript must fly over before it can get published, it may be time to check and see if you have the Author's Ego necessary for you to become an author. If so, you will know that your manuscript is the exception. It *will* be read and *it will be* published; getting it read by a publisher is just one more step in proving to others what you already know—that you are worthy of being an author.

You will solace yourself with the knowledge that others, many not as worthy, have cleared this first hurdle. Perhaps Darwin would have argued that nature has put this one more final obstacle there to cull out the weaklings, so that only the strong survive. It is the last dam in the river the salmon must leap over to reach their nesting ground; a final test that determines which fish is strong enough for nature's purpose.

A fact that should give you encouragement is that a very large portion of those manuscripts that float in and out of the editorial office sometimes read, sometimes returned unopened, are the same dog-eared submissions—the repeatedly resubmitted product of stubborn, unqualified illiterates. It is as though some turgid, odorous mass of seaweed floats into the publisher's office on the full tide, back to the sender on the ebb, the pages and packages that hold them worn and decrepit, easily recognized for what they are.

But there are ways to get your manuscript read by an editor. I'll reveal some, and you may be able to think up your own.

The simplest way is to address a letter to the editor in chief of the publishing house of your choice.

If possible address your letter to an editor by name. As an author you should be ingenious enough to learn the name of an editor; but to give you a hint of how this may be done, there may be books in your public or college library that contain this information. Particularly, there is a large, paperbound book called *LMP: Literary Market Place/Directory Of American Book Publishing*. This is published annually and lists every publisher in the United States with their addresses and also lists the names of responsible editors in these companies. It is published by R. R. Bowker Company, 1180 Avenue of the Americas, N.Y., N.Y. 10036, and is expensive.

Editors are human, and a letter addressed to one by name will be read.

The trick is to write a short letter that will make this editor have a desire to read your novel or book. You must pique his interest, then ask permission to submit the manuscript to him personally.

This letter of inquiry is a procedure requested by many publishers, and there are good reasons why this simple procedure works. If you are one of those likely to submit a manuscript on "Candy as a Cure for Cancer," "Ways to End World War I," or "Was Hitler Moses Reincarnated?," you may get a short no-interest reply, or no answer at all.

If your letter reflects sincerity and intelligence or states that you are a reporter, a teacher, an author of magazine pieces, or even a prostitute with something new in the Happy Hooker department, you will probably be asked to submit the manuscript. In asking for a look the editor has committed himself to the hope that you have something he wants.

Don't ever forget that the editor's hunger to buy is every bit as real as your hunger to sell.

If the editor rejects the manuscript, he will probably give you some word as to why. It is from such criticisms that you can learn and be encouraged to keep trying. Now, too, you have a personal contact for further submissions on the basis, "Sorry you didn't like the last one, but thanks for the helpful criticism. Here's another."

Perhaps you can evolve a better method of getting your manuscript read; but if your natural ingenuity lies in the direction of decorating the envelope with colored ribbons or including a homemade chocolate cake in a box with the manuscript, don't bother to read further in this book.

THE VERY BEST WAY TO SUBMIT A MANUSCRIPT

The preferred way to submit a book manuscript is through an agent. A submission from an established agent will be eagerly greeted. The editor's nose may even twitch slightly in anticipation as he nibbles at the first page. An agent's submission is greeted by the editor as coming from a brother professional. In submitting the manuscript the agent has indicated he believes the book is publishable or the author is a candidate to be encouraged.

Someday you—if a successful author—will have an agent. The service he renders will be worth all of the ten percent of your earnings he will collect. So get one as soon as you can, but do not expect, unless you are lucky, adroit, or connected by blood ties, to get one before you make your first book sale or have an offer to purchase your book.

It is the same story over again; the successful agent cannot afford to hunt for clients by reading manuscripts of all would-be authors. However, some agents will respond to the same kind of letter you might write an editor, and all worthwhile agents are listed in *Literary Market Place*, mentioned earlier.

One agent solicits unpublished manuscripts and will give a critical evaluation for a hundred-dollar fee. If he believes it suited for publication, he will attempt to sell the manuscript, for an agent's commission. I know of one author who started this way, but I do not recommend it. However, if you enjoy glowing comments about your work and can afford the $100 you pay to have your ego stroked, such a service may be for you. The young sincere inexperienced editor-readers will never speak harshly of your work or offend in any way the source that might dry up those hundred-dollar fees.

The most valuable agents are those who were successful editors, and many agents were. Such an agent can be of professional help to you in shaping a book or suggesting revisions or other fixing before submitting it to an editor in a position to buy, who may be—and I hope he is—one of your agent's friends. The agent, as an adversary in your behalf, may be expected to get a better contract for you than you might get for yourself in such areas as rights retained, term of contract, method of payment for tax saving, advertising commitments by the publisher for your book, and so on. His knowledge of the business assures you of all manner of protection and assistance.

If you find a publisher who wants to buy your manuscript before you find an agent willing to take you on, I advise you to engage an agent at this point to act for you in approving the first book contract and to represent you in the future. Your editor will nominate agents for you to select from, but only if you ask him. He will suggest several for you to make your choice from, because he would not want to compromise himself in any way by suggesting only one.

Will your agent negotiate a million-dollar contract on your first book?

Not a chance. Not even if yours is destined to parallel or be larger than any of those author success stories I have deliberately related to agitate your avarice and drive you determinedly to your typewriter.

The first contract will be for a modest amount. Your agent, with his knowledge of the market and his desire to strengthen your relations with the publisher, will try to get all the advance he thinks you are entitled to, but not so much as to intimidate the publisher. Rather, the agent will build acceleration clauses into your contract, giving you a higher rate of royalty at various sales levels; in this way your profit will increase, as your publisher's profit increases, as more books are sold. He will suggest what experience has dictated is the proper division of subsidiary rights between you and the publisher, including the all-important paperback rights; in short, do the things he is capable of doing expertly in his profession and leaving you to do your author thing. Some agents even function as business managers and will do your tax work. It is with the second and succeeding contracts that your agent can most effectively increase your take.

How much advance money should you expect on your first novel?

There is no pat answer because so much depends on the facts and circumstances. Let's take a particular case, a first novel by Peter Benchley.

Peter had written some magazine pieces, and these had attracted the admiration and attention of Doubleday editor, Tom Congdon. He smelled a possible book author so he invited Peter to lunch on June 4, 1971, to discuss his doing a nonfiction book. Then after learning young Benchley had just returned from Bermuda, diving there for sunken ships for the *National Geographic*, Tom inquired if Peter had ever thought of writing fiction.

"As a matter of fact I have," Ted Morgan in *The New York Times* reported Benchley as saying. "I've been thinking about a novel about a great white shark that appears off a Long Island resort and afflicts it."

Congdon asked Benchley to put the idea for his novel in a single-page outline, and on the basis of that outline and Congdon's respected professional enthusiasm, Doubleday finally agreed to advance Peter $1,000 for an option to see four chapters; and if these were satisfactory a final contract would be worked out. If not satisfactory Benchley would keep the $1,000.

Awarding an advance of $1,000 to an author who had never written a novel is most unusual, and it is a tribute to Peter's agent that it was agreed to by Doubleday, although not immediately. The fact that Peter had been published in magazines probably worked in his favor, as did the fact that his father, Nathaniel Benchley, is a successful writer and novelist, and his grandfather was the famous humorist Robert Benchley. It may be the first time editor Congdon was influenced in placing a bet on blood lines away from the track, but it paid off.

Nine months later, after intensive rewriting and revision of the first four chapters under Congdon's direction, he wrote Benchley: "I'm delighted we're going to do your book." The contract department approved a $7,500 advance: $1,000 for the option already paid, $2,500 on signing the contract, $2,000 on delivery of the first draft, and $2,000 on acceptance of the final manuscript. Benchley now started writing in earnest.

The writing eventually totaled two complete and several partial rewrites before the final draft was turned in on January 2, 1973. The first discussion on the fiction story concerning a shark between Congdon and Benchley had taken place June 4, 1971, just about nineteen months before.

The first tangible indication of the birth of a big best-seller came when Bantam bought paperback rights for an advance, against royalty earned on sales, of $575,000. Advances from three book clubs came in quickly for a total of $85,000, as did advances of more than $100,000 for foreign publishing rights. A motion picture sale was made to the producing company of Brown-Zanuck for a guarantee of $100,000 for the author, and possibly more movie income as the contract specified a percent of the profits to go to the author if the gross profit from the picture exceeded a certain, and rather astronomical, figure. This provision for a percent of the gross profit to go to the author is somewhat unusual in movie contracts and is usually reserved for a very famous author or a widely competed-for publishing property, and such was not the case for *Jaws* at that early date. It was fortunate for Peter, as you shall see, that his agent, International Creative Management, secured this share-of-the-profits clause for their young, first-novel client. They also got Peter a contract to write the screenplay for $25,000. He did that job over three times.

Now that some book sale figures are available, and from information and estimates gathered from experienced persons in book publishing, here is a reasonable, "ball park" estimate of what Peter has earned from book publications in about two years:

Hardcover (U.S.A.)	$ 300,000
Paperback (U.S.A.)	1,500,000
(Peter probably got the standard 50% of total paperback royalty of about $3,000,000)	
Foreign, all languages, hard- and soft-cover	600,000
Book Clubs	200,000

From this estimated total of $2,600,000 Peter will have paid his agent $260,000, leaving him almost $2,400,000 from book earnings alone, and this will get larger as time passes and more copies are sold.

Now, what about motion picture earnings for the author?

There was, you will remember, a guarantee of $100,000 for movie rights, plus $25,000 for writing the screenplay, and the clause in the contract giving Peter an additional percentage of the picture's gross profit, exceeding the very high originally defined gross profit figure.

Now I can rejoice with you that it is an undisputed, handclapping fact for authors everywhere that Peter's "share of the profits" has brought him checks in a period of less than two years since the picture's release, totaling more than $8 million.

Thus, author Benchley has received, net, from book and movie revenue something more than $10 million from *Jaws*. And this figure will grow steadily, particularly from the repeated re-releases of the movie and its eventual multimillion-dollar sale to TV. It seems certain that eventual earnings for Peter from the movie alone will exceed $10 million.

Total earnings for the author from this one book may reach $15 million, more than has been paid any professional sports hero for a single effort, I am pleased to report. And, wryly, more than the combined lifetime earnings of his famous author-and-humorist grandfather, Robert Benchley, and his successful novelist father, Nathaniel.

While Peter's is the exceptional case, and must represent the most money ever made by an author from a single book, the very fact that this one book of popular, contemporary fiction can earn such an enormous amount for the author, is a compelling indication that other books, as yet unwritten, can also break earning and popularity records, and that publishing has, truly, new and ever-growing profit opportunities for authors.

So, you are probably not going to write another *Jaws*, and you, if a first-time author, will most likely have to produce the completed first draft of a novel before you can expect any advance money.

What kind of money reward can you expect?

The greatest early reward you should expect might be the chance to do some rewriting to the editor's satisfaction, leading to possible acceptance and a contract. If rewriting and revision is suggested, do it. Unless you need the money badly I would suggest you work with the editor without any advance at this point, hoping you can complete the manuscript in a fashion that leads him to say, "We want to buy it."

Then you can talk about an advance or, if you agree with my earlier advice, bring in an agent to make the deal.

If the editor insists on an option agreement before he works with you on revision, be satisfied with anything he offers as an advance. It may be five hundred dollars or even less. If the option is a simple one that does not specify royalty rates on the finished novel and any details beyond: "The author agrees to prepare further drafts and should the final draft be acceptable to the publisher, enter into a publishing contract at terms to be mutually agreed upon," sign it. However, if the contract specifies terms and further conditions for publication, get an agent at this point.

If your submitted manuscript is in final form, or nearly so, when the publisher wants to buy and you have no agent, I don't think your advance should be less than $1,500. If the publisher is much impressed he may offer you more: $5,000, $7,500, or $10,000.

While publishers resist paying more than necessary, they also have a built-in sense of fairness and most are smart enough not to take advantage of an author. Indeed, he is someone they hope to build a profitable, harmonious relationship with.

Again, under any circumstances in which you can bring in an agent to negotiate for you, do so. This will not be resented by the publisher. He may balk if the agent is brought in too early, but he should not object at the point when he wants to buy your book or offers you a contract.

The above estimates of what you might be offered in cash for your book are presented in an effort to answer a question I am sure is on your mind. I dared to put down some figures but I cannot guarantee, or do other than guess, what you might be offered in payment.

Okay, you have sold your book with or without an agent. It is going to be published. You have signed a contract. You have an advance payment against royalties. What follows?

The book will become a reality in your hands in the bookstores in about a year. *Jaws* was published in January 1974. The manuscript was finished and accepted in January 1973.

Between acceptance and publication many things have happened to your manuscript and you. You did some rewriting at your own and your editor's suggestion. This took a week—or was it six months? Then final editing by your editor, and final-final editing by the firm's copy editor.

Publishing plans had to be made far ahead so that your book could be glowingly described, displayed, and pictured in the publisher's catalog. The catalog itself must be available several months in advance of publication to bookstores, jobbers, and the publisher's own salesmen. This is so that your book may be ordered, shipped, and placed on sale, probably three weeks or so before the advertised on-sale date. This jumping of release date will give ample time for book reviewers to get the reviews in print while the book is certain to be available on dealers' shelves. A review too far in advance is wasted. Earlier, a proper slot had to be found on the publisher's seasonal list for your book, a slot in the traditional fall or spring list that does not have a too-similar book. Publicity plans had to be coordinated. Your book had to be set in type, and proof sheets pulled for you to read and make the final corrections before the book was printed and bound.

Then your publisher will ask your help in publicizing the book, first in your own community. Nothing creates such a favorable stir—one that may grow into a tidal wave of publicity—as the news

74

that a local citizen has published a book. If the book is liked the information spreads by some chain of magic. Apparently the new author's neighbor, impressed by the book and proud to know an author, writes words to that effect to her cousin in St. Louis, and that cousin, equally pleased, sends word to her daughter in Alaska, etc., etc., etc. Each one in the chain, hopefully and magically, buys the book or persuades someone to buy the book and talk about it. All agree it is the chain-letter effect of person talking to person about a book that sells it.

If your book is judged by the publisher to have best-seller potential and you are judged to have a "merchandisable personality," you may be asked to address the company's salesmen, assembled in meetings, to whip up their enthusiasm. The publicity staff will take you by the hand, coach you for publicity appearances, and fling you into a nationwide publicity tour. Coast to coast you go, crisscrossing the country, exhausted but loving every part of it, speaking to women's clubs, Lions, Rotary, librarians, newspaper feature writers; appearing on local radio, local TV, national radio, national TV—particularly the network talk shows, *Today*, *Merv Griffin*, and others. There will be some autograph-signing parties in big bookstores. The publisher's inventive flacks will put you in an iron cage submerged deep in the ocean where you will be shown photographing great white sharks for the benefit of TV cameras and the resultant extra sales of your book—if your name is Peter Benchley and you have written a book called *Jaws*.

This kind of frenzied "pump it up" merchandising costs the publisher money and, along with national newspaper and TV advertising of books, is a new result of the publishing industry's having recently discovered that the public, while starving for books, must be told of their availability.

Along with elaborate and expensive publicity efforts, publishers are spending, for the first time, large amounts to advertise single books. An advertising budget of $100,000 was decided upon for *Jaws* before publication, and this amount was increased as the book sales took off. Newspaper ads of a modest sort have been used by publishers for many years, but now radio and TV time is being purchased by both hardcover and paperback publishers in amounts that may exceed a quarter of a million dollars on a single book.

This phenomenon of dramatically increased merchandising efforts is, I hope, of personal interest to anyone who may be weighing a decision as to whether to become an author or to enter the publishing business in any way.

The simple, distilled fact is that the American public has been found to have a far greater desire for books, and willingness to pay for them, than was ever before known.

The publicity and advertising programs have been developed because the desire for books exists. It is not that advertising and promotion has made a market.

This fact of the reader's hunger for books is obvious from your personal observation, as well as from sales statistics. Simply ask yourself if there is anything you enjoy more, or can count on to more certainly please, then a really good book.

What will turn heads faster in a gathering of people than an enthusiastic voice, "I've just read the best book!"

It is the function of all book advertising to spread that message in one form or another.

And for those of you who like the statistical picture:

TV book advertising in 1972 totaled a little under $2,000,000.

TV book advertising doubled in 1973 to $4,200,000.

TV book advertising jumped to $9,000,000 in 1974.

Newspapers carried $20,000,000 of national book advertising in 1974. That is the figure spent by publishers and does not include retail ads.

SOME STUFF YOU DON'T KNOW

If you were contemplating some profession other than writing as a career, no matter what—from merchandising to medicine, law, or teaching—you would, as part of your training, be exposed to its history and development.

You won't find any history of authorship. You can find some histories of publishing, but they are of more interest to those who wrote them than to the students who are required to read them.

As an author you will profit from knowing, because of the security it promises writers, some of the facts that led up to this burgeoning bonanza of seemingly limitless book sales.

Will this insatiable appetite for books last? To get the answer let's go back, briefly, to how book publishing started in this country.

It had its birth in the printing of political pamphlets, as published by Jefferson, Franklin, Paine, and others, to inform those relatively few who could read about political events and theories of the day; and to spur rebellion and the Revolutionary War.

Education for reading was limited and slow to spread. Production of bound books for the public, including textbooks, books on law, and books on medicine, was very small until after the Civil War. The classics were the possessions of the gentry, usually printed in England and imported in small quantity, and mostly given as gifts, frequently to families where only one person or none could read.

And that was not long ago, as time is measured. The war was from 1861 to 1865.

A few publishers founded prior to the Civil War are still in business, including Harper, now Harper & Row, and G. P. Putnam's Sons. After the war more American book publishers crept into being, but with little emphasis on popular reading except in the case of the dime novel. These early paperbacks had their greatest flowering in the thirty years following the Civil War, until 1895. The American book of quality had an enthusiastic but small following and was represented by Howells, Twain, James, Longfellow's poems, and *Uncle Tom's Cabin*. For such books to sell more than a few thousand copies was a rare exception and required a period of years.

But the appetite for reading was there and growing!

Then, really very recently, printing of books became more than a slow, cumbersome hand-manufacture operation. Presses and book binderies were invented that could lower costs and speed production to feed the hunger for reading that had been stimulated by a network of public and private schools. Then school attendance became compulsory through the upper grades, and the "mechanical age" required books of a technical sort for engineers, teachers, lawyers, doctors, and all the professions.

Suddenly reading became a part of nearly everyone's daily life, and as each person read, for whatever reason, he found reading in itself a great satisfaction. Reading was a blood-stirring, laugh-provoking, emotion-churning experience. Books became a magic world of fantasy into which the reader could retreat from a rough and often cruel world.

This was the period, from the turn of the century and preceding World War II, when the circulation of national magazines spurted.

The Saturday Evening Post, claiming kinship to Benjamin Franklin's pamphlet dating back to 1821, did not really become a genuine national magazine until after 1880. In 1897 when Horace Lorimer became its most famous editor, it became, for its day, a large circulation periodical. *Collier's* was founded in 1888 and it too became a large circulation periodical that did a considerable part in stimulating readership by the general public.

As a further stimulation to reading and directly as a result of the public hunger for reading, public libraries were started in many communities, including those founded by Andrew Carnegie. This availability of books, too expensive for most to buy, served to encourage readers—to make hungry addicts of them—each searching for more to read.

Prior to World War I there were fewer than five hundred bookstores in the United States, stores depending in any substantial part on the sale of books. My uncle, Harry Barker, owned the one store in Springfield, Illinois, capital of the state, that deserved the name of bookstore in the early 1900s. Business was not so bustling that he wasn't able to take care of me, as a small child, in his store while my mother went shopping. Indeed, in vest and visor he served all of that sizable city's book buyers single-handed, his other few employees occupied with picture framing, selling school supplies, prints, and what my father called "uncle Harry's gold mine."

This consisted of two-inch-square pieces of wood, on which was printed with a rubber stamp the information that what the purchaser held in his hand had once been part of the flooring of President Lincoln's first law office, which had been in Springfield.

Uncle Harry owned a bookstore because it gave him the opportunity to read almost everything in stock, relatively undisturbed. His was the desk back of the stacks through which he could peek and survey the entire store. Never would he emerge to serve customers unless he was sure it was a book they wanted to buy.

So aloof was he from physical labor that he had time to dream up a variety of charming schemes, one of which—the Lincoln's office-flooring bit—was very successful. It is not true, I'm quite sure, that he persuaded the owner of the building that housed Lincoln's first law office to permit him to replace the worn floorboards at his expense with new flooring, and take in exchange the old boards "for kindling." Rather, I believe some small alteration was made in the office which resulted in a few boards of flooring being replaced. Uncle Harry obtained these. The mystery was how so few boards could produce so many two-inch-square mementos to be sold at the then-high price of one dollar each. It is true he never displayed more than two pieces at a time in a secure and locked glass case on top of his counter, much as Cartier might display diamonds; but clerks in the picture-framing department were reported by jealous merchants to spend much of their spare time cutting old boards into small pieces.

After World War I, books began to sell in greater, but still small, quantities. The merchandising of these items, so often of timely and therefore perishable content, encountered more problems than did the selling of almost anything else the public bought, from dry goods to wet goods. Books took up space, had a small profit markup, and required an impossibly large stock if the retailer was to meet the request for any published book a customer might order. The dealer could order a book for a customer, but weeks or even months would pass before he could deliver it.

Indeed, the merchandising situation was a classic one to which there seemed no solution for the bookseller. Demand was not great enough to warrant expenses and investment entailed in keeping a large stock. The buyers seemed to want either hard-to-obtain or just-recently published books. High prices contributed to keeping the dependable book-buying public discouragingly small.

Then came a solution. A solution that solved some of the problems the publishers and retailers of books had not been able to solve. A way was found to supply books to readers, fast and for less than was usually charged by the bookstore. The solution was the book club. Books by mail at bargain prices. Sometimes for ten cents in the "come on" offer, often free. This solution was no solution for the book retailer and only a partial solution for the book publisher, who found himself in a situation where someone else—owners of the book club—would make more profit from his product than he did. The solution did serve the book reader. That is why it succeeded. He could order a book of his choice and get it quickly, sometimes before the bookstore. By joining a club he could be sure of a steady supply of books conveniently delivered to his home. No need to go miles to search through the stock of a bookstore for something to read and run the risk that the store did not have the book he wanted.

Prior to World War II there were fewer than two thousand bookstores in the United States, but dozens of book clubs and other mail-order booksellers.

Then another merchandising revolution in the business—born because the book industry was not supplying enough books cheaply—the paperback books!

Pocket Books was the first paperback trade mark in this country, followed soon by others. The low-price paperback was launched in the United States in 1939, and its growth in sales stifled further the growth of regular bookstores. As late as 1972–73 there were fewer than thirty-five hundred retail bookstores for hardcover books, although low-price paperback books were selling millions of copies a month. Thus it was demonstrated that readership of books had increased steadily and dramatically to heights never dreamed of.

So huge did individual book sales become in this period, 1965-72, that one fiction book sold more copies in those few years than had ever been sold of one novel since the invention of printing. *The Godfather* by Mario Puzo, an unknown author, racked up more than fifteen million sales in the English language alone, almost entirely in paperback.

Most of the sales of the thousands of titles suddenly available in low prices in paperback were being achieved through the nationwide distribution system that had grown up to handle magazine sales. Independent wholesalers in all except small cities were handling large geographic areas with truck delivery to retailers. Then book jobbers started handling paperbacks, servicing specialized retail accounts in competition with wholesalers. Some of these jobbers had handled hardcover books, but many sprang up to handle paperbacks alone.

Retail outlets for paperbacks are being opened in all communities today. No one is sure how many such paperback bookstores there are, but they are estimated at about 80,000 and are growing fast.

A peculiarity of the situation is that five years ago the number of retail paperback outlets was estimated at about 100,000. The greater share of these stores were small establishments that carried a few hundred titles in a hard-to-find rack. Today this type of operation is being forced out of business by the larger store with a stock of thousands of paperback titles. Thus the estimated 80,000 paperback outlets today are selling vastly more copies than the possible 100,000 stores of five years ago.

Some wholesale agency owners operate and personally own as many as a dozen or more retail paperback stores in their territory, and they also service hundreds of other paperback retailers through a truck delivery operation or by mail. These agencies also service schools—many of which have their own paperback bookstores—and libraries.

And all of this has become possible as the public has demonstrated a willingness to pay more than the bargain price of twenty-five cents originally charged for paperbacks. This low price was the opening wedge, but the service being given to readers now: the many stores, efficient trucks, and the expensive shipping and handling of large quantities of paperbacks could not be accomplished at super-low book prices. It was when the public demonstrated a willingness to pay more than one dollar for a paperback—as much for a good book as they pay for a movie or a haircut—that American merchandising know-how took over. Now the business is booming and can only go up.

Large paperback book sections are appearing in thousands of supermarkets and, with books competing for space and nudging food off the shelves of a supermarket, you as an interested author-to-be can be sure books are here to stay.

The paperback bookstore is now present in almost every high-traffic center. Book buyers throng them and know they can very likely find the book they want at what is still a relatively low price for value given. The traffic in these paperback bookstores has resulted in the beginning of another revolutionary and surprising bookselling development: The paperback bookstores are stocking increasing numbers of "trade paperbacks"—three or four dollar books that in many cases are printed from the original plates of the hardcover book. Off-size quality paperbacks on fine art subjects, hobbies, and so on are being sold in these stores in ever larger numbers at figures, in some cases, of more than 500,000 copies. And then, the almost unbelievable:

As these numerous paperback stores sell more and more high-price paperbacks, some of these stores are finding it profitable to display a sizable stock of hardcover books and sell them to book buyers not willing to wait a year or more for the cheaper paperback editions.

It would seem that finally the hardcover publisher, the guy responsible for books in the first place, buffeted by lack of retail book outlets and by marketing conditions he couldn't cope with, forced to watch paperback publishers and mail-order operators make more profit than he did from his property, may be coming into the position publishers of hardcovers believe they are entitled to. It just may be that hardcover books will now be displayed in many thousands of retail stores instead of in just a select few, dragged into widespread retail exposure by the public demand for cheaper books that is responsible for the blossoming outlets for paperbacks.

The point of most importance to you is that the rapid expansion of retail book outlets, with the resultant more satisfying service to book buyers, means still more good and salable books will be needed to service reader demand at these now numerous retail outlets.

So get busy. Write your book.

If you need more evidence that book authorship is a promising, growing, and always-to-be-with-us profession, let's take a quick peek into the future: The latest reliable forecast of population growth in the United States says our citizenry will increase beyond the 1970 figure of 202 million to 248 million by 1985, just about a twenty-five percent increase in a short 15 years. By the year 2000 our population will be 287 million.

That represents a great many more readers in a very few years, and they will demand many, many more books per reader than today's population because of increased education, older median age, and other factors.

It might seem—unless somebody or something starts poking a great many people in the eyes with sharp sticks—all the pulp forests

81

in the world will not supply the paper needed to meet the demand for books.

Another development that will give you further assurance that the business of being a book author has to be an expanding business is the quite recent entry of the "makers and shakers" of the communication world into book publishing. I am referring to the entry of Radio Corporation of America (RCA) and Columbia Broadcasting System (CBS).

This amounts to a radical and new amalgamation of radio and television with book publishing by two giants of the communication world unwilling to be in publishing previously because they felt the profit potential too small.

CBS plunged in when they bought the old and prestigious trade book, technical, juvenile, religious, and educational publisher, Holt Rinehart and Winston. Then they quickly acquired two paperback lines, Popular Library and Collier Books. Now more recently, CBS has signed an agreement to buy the company I was associated with for so long, Fawcett Publications. No doubt CBS appreciates the famous magazines they are getting with this acquisition, *Woman's Day, Mechanix Illustrated, Rudder,* etc., but the Fawcett properties that really prompted the purchase were the line of Fawcett paperbacks, Crest, Gold Medal, Premier, and the nearly forty-year-old nationwide distribution system for books and magazines. Thus, CBS will be among the largest publishers and distributors of paperback books. Yes indeed, CBS is spending millions in recognition that book publishing is BIG BUSINESS and getting bigger.

RCA acquired two of the real giants of hardcover publishing, Random House and Alfred A. Knopf. With the former they also acquired Vintage Books and Modern Library. They have since purchased a paperback line, Ballantine Books.

This sudden rush to success by the book business has brought another important segment of the communications industry into publishing, the Hollywood moviemakers. Warner Communications, parent company of Warner Brothers, the movie company, is in the paperback business through acquisition of Paperback Library, an old and lagging paperback firm Warners is pumping money and life into.

Warner is bringing circus publicity, which has always accompanied movie merchandising, to paperback selling. This company claims to have spent as much as a quarter of a million dollars on TV advertising for a single book. Their aggressive bidding and publicity stunts have stimulated the whole industry.

More recently Gulf and Western, owners of Paramount Pictures, has acquired the old longtime successful publishing firm of

Simon and Schuster and with it Pocket Books, oldest of the American paperback lines, which had also fallen on hard times in recent years as many of their competitors passed them by in sales and profits.

Not only are the moguls of Hollywood interested in the profits they expect from becoming book publishers, but they have a dream of owning the whole pig—bacon, ham, sausage, ribs, tail, and all. Films have always been dependent on story material, since the first step in successful film producing is the acquisition of a good story. Hollywood has found that successful books, best-sellers, are the most surefire material for movies. Now as owners of book publishing companies, Warners and Paramount have in mind buying film rights, reprint rights, book rights, popcorn rights, and all other rights to an author's material at the moment it comes out of the typewriter.

But it won't work that way. Owning these publishing companies will give Warners and Paramount an opportunity to be closer to the author whose story they may eventually own for book publication and want for movie use; that's all. The author's agent will not permit these falcons of the film companies to fly away with the film rights at bargain rates. They will continue to be sold to the movie producer willing to pay the highest price.

Another circumstance that has attracted the filmmakers to book publishing is the discovery that hardcover and paperback publishers have been willing to pay considerable money, in some instances, for the privilege of turning a screenplay into a novel. *Love Story* and *Summer of Forty-two* are examples of novels that were written after, and from, the screenplay and sold enormously well as books. In neither case did the film companies get as much of the book profit as they would have liked, in view of the novel's having been written from their property, the screenplay. However, it's doubtful that the Screen Writers' Guild, the Authors' League, or authors' agents will stand by while Hollywood welds shackles and leg irons on authors and herds them into slave compounds. No, sir, not as long as an author has an agent and a free choice will he end up with the short end of the money stick. He will always have a choice as to which publisher publishes his work.

Still it's nice to have all that promotion activity and sudden competitive stirring in an industry that is completely, entirely, absolutely, irrevocably, dependent upon the author.

Do you need any more convincing that authorship is the business to be in?

You say you want some statistics, not just fancy prose, not names like Warner Brothers, Paramount Pictures, RCA, and CBS thrown blindingly into your eyes while you are led helpless to a typewriter and told to turn out the great American novel? You say you want the clincher?

Okay, here are a few statistics, but very few, and they are for the United States only.

In 1974 there was a total of 30,575 new books published. This was an increase of eight percent over the 28,140 published in the previous year and an increase of nearly fourteen percent over 1972.

At this rate of growth the book industry might expect to double the number of titles published in just about ten years!

It won't happen that way though because there simply are not enough qualified writers to turn out that many books of a quality that would guarantee sales. Do you get the point?

Seriously, there are other factors that would motivate against doubling the number of titles published in the next ten-year period, but there is no doubt the production and sales pattern for books is up, and the demand for writers is go, go, go!

Another skinny statistic or two about fiction: In 1972 there were 2,109 new fiction titles, mostly in hardcover. In 1974 there were 2,382 new fiction books. This did not include juvenile books, a large part of the fiction market. In 1972 there were 2,126 juvenile books. In 1974 there were 2,336 juvenile books.

Statistics on mass paperbacks are not as reliable as those on hardcover books, but the best available from *Publishers Weekly*, the source for the hardcover book statistics also, show the number of new paperback titles in 1974 to be 1,263. In 1973 new titles reported totaled 988, and in 1972 they totaled 824. That is a very fast growth rate.

Total mass-market paperback titles printed in 1974, including reissues of titles originally published in previous years, are given as 2,802, with an explanation that figures on mass-market paperbacks are so unreliable, so difficult to assemble accurately, that the figure of 2,802 may be low by *as many as 1,500 titles!* This could bring the total of mass-market paperback titles printed in 1974 to about 4,300, and this is closer to the true figure than the 2,802 on which records are available.

The following list of the number of new books published in 1974 is interesting because it defines the categories, twenty-four of them, in which authors have chosen to write and publishers to publish, as well as the number of books published in each category.

The totals do not include all of the original paperback titles. For that reason the totals, particularly fiction, are low by as much as forty percent.

CLASSIFICATION	NEW BOOKS
Agriculture	299
Art	1,220
Biography	1,380
Business	732
Education	963
Fiction	2,382
General Works	872
History	801
Home Economics	666
Juveniles	2,336
Language	315
Law	743
Literature	1,304
Medicine	1,799
Music	172
Philosophy, Psychology	1,003
Poetry, Drama	1,155
Religion	1,458
Science	2,574
Sociology, Economics	5,068
Sports, Recreation	839
Technology	1,298
Travel	1,196
TOTALS	30,575

The following table shows the number of new titles and new editions of older books for each five-year period since 1950. This table shows in an even more dramatic statistical way how rapidly the book industry is growing. The estimated number of titles is low, but it is not possible to say how low.

YEAR	NO. OF TITLES	PERCENT INCREASE
1950	11,022	
1955	12,589	10
1960	15,012	12
1965	28,595	51
1970	36,071	26
1973	39,851	11

A TALE TO STIR
APPLAUSE AND ENVY

Enough statistics. Let's speed on to something far more interesting, a dramatic story that should interest writers everywhere and might well be entitled:

> *How One Author Succeeded in Selling a Novel His Publisher Did Not Want and Saw His Unwanted Book Become the Largest-Selling Novel Ever Published; And in So Doing Brought Great Happiness and Great Wealth to Some and Great Sorrow to Others.*

I happen to be among those who were brought great happiness when Fawcett published the paperback edition. Putnam was brought great happiness because that company published the hardcover edition. Francis Ford Coppola, who produced the picture for Paramount, felt great joy, but none to compare with that which befell the author, Mario Puzo. The book is *The Godfather*.

Mario tells the story of his writing this record breaker of all novels in great and interesting detail in his book, *The Godfather Papers*. As an observer and sideline participant, I can contribute a few additional details, one of which is that movie revenue from *The Godfather* has topped $125 million, more than was ever grossed by a picture, and it is still going up, although it is destined to be topped by *Jaws*.

But back to Mario. As an author he had written two previous novels, *The Fortunate Pilgrim* and *Dark Arena*, both published to significant lack of success by Atheneum. Both are splendid novels and both achieved high sales when republished after Mario's name became famous as author of *The Godfather*.

So the day came when he desired a signed contract and a $5,000 advance for a third novel he proposed to write. That was the day he presented a short outline and several chapters of a novel to be called *The Godfather* to Atheneum, as specified in the option clause of his previous contract. His publisher, Atheneum, had first opportunity to publish for the $5,000 advance Mario requested. The answer from Atheneum was no, on the basis of poor sales for the two previous books.

No publisher it seemed was interested in this novel of the Mafia family; many publishers turned down the opportunity to buy or to make an offer.

This state of affairs made Mario impatient. Mario knew the novel would be good, even as his author-ego told him his previous

86

two novels had been good. There actually had been a third novel of his authorship that he would agree had not been good. He had met this situation by publishing it under a pseudonym.

At this point, in 1964, G.P. Putnam's Sons, Fawcett paperbacks, McCall's magazine and Joe Levine's Embassy Pictures had joined hands and funds to conduct a story contest at the suggestion of Putnam editor, William Targ. A total of $410,000 was being guaranteed, with larger earnings assured, for book rights, magazine rights and motion picture rights for an unpublished novel judged suited to the four mediums.

The submissions for such a paltry guarantee had not been many or promising when a junior editor at Putnam mentioned to Senior Editor Bill Targ that somebody named Mario Puzo had a Mafia novel that might work.

"Have him submit it," Bill suggested.

In a few days Mario came in, without even the outline he had shown Atheneum, but hoping to enter the contest.

"Too bad," said Targ. "The deadline is two weeks away and only completed manuscripts are eligible."

Mario replied he was not prepared to knock out a novel in two weeks. Targ, an editor possessed with an insatiable hunger for publishable books encouraged Mario to tell him about the proposed novel, and was favorably enough impressed to pay $1200 of Putnam money down, with a promise of more money at the half-way mark, and the balance of a $5000 advance to be paid when the manuscript was finished.

This encouraged Mario to quit his editing job on an adventure magazine so that he would have more time to write. Three years later he had completed the Mafia manuscript. During the three years he supported his family writing magazine pieces and a children's book. He got some money from Paramount Pictures, too. This came about when he had about one hundred pages of the Mafia novel in manuscript form, attempted to pry more advance money out of Targ and failed. Targ did suggest a motion picture company might be willing to come through with some money at this point. At Mario's urging he submitted the one hundred available pages, as yet untitled, and lightning struck. A perspective gent in the Paramount story department, Marvin Birdt by name, saw in the few pages a theme and a value that might overcome all the obstacles inherent in the long steeplechase from manuscript pages, to film-in-the-can, then, possibly, to a successful movie. Paramount offered an option payment of $12,500.00 against a total of $50,000 for movie rights with "escalators" if they exercised the option. Mario's agent, the William

Morris Company, advised against accepting. They suggested Mario wait. "That," said Mario, "was like advising a guy under water to take a deep breath. I needed the cash and $12,500 looked like Fort Knox." He didn't wait.

The manuscript finally in hand, Targ gave Mario the last payment of $1200.00 due. Mario took the money and ran. He ran to Europe with his family, having promised his wife this would be the year she would see her family after a twenty-year absence. They did the grand tour on credit cards and the $1200.00. While abroad Mario received a list of proposed titles, one of which was The Godfather, and that was the title Mario selected. When the Puzos hit these shores again Mario owed the credit card companies $8000.00 and now says, "I wasn't worried. If worse came to worse we could always sell our house. Or I could go to jail. Hell, better writers have gone to jail. No sweat."

Ms. Leona Nevler, then editor of Fawcett Crest Books, heard of the manuscript at Putnam and asked to read it for possible reprint purchase. She read it quickly and sent it to me at Nantucket Island, where I was vacationing. Hers was an enthusiastic report and contained the comment: "This could sell a million copies in reprint."

I had picked up the manuscript in its envelope at the Siasconset post office on the way home from the golf course, and read Leona's enthusiastic report while enjoying a gin and tonic. I respect her judgment and her hunches, so I put the manuscript aside only long enough to eat a sandwich for lunch, then went eagerly to reading.

Four hours later I was still sitting in my golf clothes on the porch reading one of the most compelling stories I had ever read. I had another sandwich for dinner and continued reading until I finished the manuscript just before midnight.

The next morning I called the office and told Editor Nevler my enthusiasm was even greater than hers, a judgment easier for someone to make after there has been a favorable initial report.

She told me the grapevine reported that Putnam already had a bid of $50,000 for paperback rights from Bantam. My suggestion was that I call the president of Putnam, Walter Minton, a now and then golfing companion, and attempt a close-out bid immediately over the phone. "I'll sweep Walter off his feet," was mentioned, I believe.

So I placed the call to Walter, told him I had just finished reading the manuscript and wanted to buy it for reprint.

"We've got a pretty good offer for it now," was his answering ploy. "So I heard," I countered. "It's a very good offer you have, but if I gave you a substantially bigger bid over the phone right now, would you take it?"

There was silence for a moment, then I heard Walter's famous hum, "*mmmmmmmmmmm*, it would probably depend on what you mean by 'substantial,' " he replied.

Now, I said to myself, is the time for the sweep-him-off-his-feet bit.

Then to Walter, "Suppose I offer more than twice the other offer you have? Say, $105,000."

A long silence ensued while Walter contemplated the fact that Fawcett was willing to pay a guaranteed advance of $105,000, twenty times the $5,000 he had paid Puzo. He must have been considering, too, that half of that $105,000 would be going to Putnam before their edition was published.

"Your offer is substantially more," he agreed finally. "But I will have to consult the author, and there is an agent in the deal."

Walter had not been swept off his feet.

The following day he called back with the disturbing answer that author and agent insisted the book be put out for auction, but that Fawcett would have something of a preferred position, possibly "last man out" in the bidding.

The auction spread over a period of about four days, with Walter telephoning me news of increasing interest and higher bids by several reprinters. The bids went quickly to $150,000. Would I top that? Yes.

Then to $200,000, $250,000 and, by smaller and smaller increases, to $335,000. Now there was only one other bidder left in the contest.

Finally, to climax a situation that had involved too many phone calls and was messing up my vacation, I made a final strategy bid calculated to end the bidding, win or lose.

"I'll raise the last bid of $335,000 by $50,000 to $385,000 with the agreement that I get the book for that price unless the other bidder tops me by $25,000 and will pay $410,000," was my proposal.

Walter was tired of the repeated phone calls and the pattern of small increases in bidding that the auction had taken, with my opponent raising only $1,000 or $2,000 at a time, so he accepted the "freeze-out" suggestion. He also encouraged me by stating that he did not think the unknown other bidder would go to $410,000.

He was wrong. The next morning Walter called and told me my competitor had bought the book at the price I had set, $410,000. The purchaser was Helen Meyer, president of Dell.

My vacation was not helped in its final week by losing that book. After I had been back in the office a week or so I was still shaking my head sadly at the loss when Walter called with an offer to buy lunch.

Instead I invited him to the Lambs Club, where he told me Ms. Meyer seemed to be showing evidence of cold feet on the *Godfather* deal and was insisting on one stipulation that had not been part of the original offer and, indeed, had not been mentioned previously. The condition she now advanced was that she wanted to also buy reprint rights to a second Putnam Mafia novel, *The Family* by Leslie Waller. This book was scheduled to be published by Putnam before *The Godfather* and thus it would be assumed *The Family* would be on the stands and in the stores before *The Godfather* was in paperback.

Ms. Meyer was apprehensive that the prior publication of *The Family* might take the edge off the public appetite for Mafia books if published first. Because of this she insisted on the right to buy *The Family* for reprint with an advance of $45,000 and proposed to refrain from publishing it in paperback until after *The Godfather* was published in paperback.

Walter was in a bind. Signet had already offered $50,000 for reprint rights to *The Family*. When he apprised Ms. Meyer of this, it was her suggestion that Walter make up the author's share of the $5,000 difference to author Waller out of the $410,000 she was to pay for *The Godfather*.

That's when Walter said he would think about her, for him, expensive suggestion and called me for lunch.

Not only had the deal for *The Family* with Signet been all but finalized, but also to hold back Waller's book until after *The Godfather* would be playing fast and loose with Waller's property, his rights as an author, and would possibly injure the sales of his book.

Walter asked if I would get back in *The Godfather* bidding fray and guarantee $410,000, the price Dell had indicated earlier they would pay. Would I pay that amount with no restriction on the release date of *The Family* by Signet?

Walter had swept me off my feet, and I said yes.

Subsequently, Signet paid an advance of $62,500 for paperback rights to *The Family*, $17,500 more than Ms. Meyer insisted Putnam accept from Dell.

The reprint contracts for *The Godfather* were signed and the history-making novel was launched in hardcover. The Putnam edition got so-so reviews, but the public loved the book and bought all the copies they could find. Putnam found themselves suddenly "out of stock," as happens when a book catches on quickly, and ran the presses overtime to meet the demand.

When it came time for our reprint edition more than a year after the hardcover, we ordered the largest first printing in the history of publishing, a record-breaking first printing of 3 million copies and an advertising and promotion budget of $250,000.

To date Fawcett has sold more than 10 million copies with other English language editions bringing sales over 15 million.

Mario was given $100,000, brought to Hollywood and guaranteed a tennis-playing secretary, to write the screenplay. Paramount, when they realized what a gold mine they had tapped with their early purchase of screen rights for an advance of $25,000, came through with a "piece of the picture" for the author; that is, a share in the profits at a point in its earnings that was set so high it was not expected Mario would profit hugely. So successful is the picture, however, that Mario is getting a real hunk, possibly as much as $1 million! Too, he is earning from *The Godfather, Part II*, for which he wrote the screenplay.

A further bit of information about Mario and that screenplay: When I first heard of the new project, a motion picture called *Godfather II*, I started to talk up to Mario and Francis Ford Coppola, the director, a plan to have a novel written from the screenplay. Such a book, called *Godfather II*, preceding the second motion picture and trading off of the original big-selling novel, could not fail. Two to 3 million sales in paperback at $2 each would be assured. Mario's take could be expected to be more than $500,000.

I knew Mario would not have time to write this novel after the screenplay was completed for release before the picture, so I suggested getting a competent novelist of his choice to do the job for a flat fee; the novel would be written to Mario's satisfaction or it would not be published.

"There will be no inference you wrote the novelization," I told Mario. "The credit on the cover of the book will read simply, 'from the screenplay by Mario Puzo. Novelization by Joe Whoever.' "

Mario thought it over for a few seconds. Then said, "Nothing doing. If there is a novel in any way connected with *The Godfather*, or *Godfather II*, my name will be associated with it by the public, and no novel appears with my name on it unless I write it. I agree I don't have time to write the novel, so there will be no book written called *Godfather II*."

For more than a year I kept nudging Mario, calling Coppola in

Hollywood and writing him letters urging him to help persuade Mario to change his mind, pointing out that such a book preceding *Godfather II* would be valuable publicity.

Each time I brought the matter up again Mario would politely reconsider, but each time his answer was no.

"I wouldn't be comfortable with someone else's name on a book that traded off my novel and was made from my screenplay," he insisted.

Mario had been satisfied with a cash advance of $1,500 on *The Godfather*, but wouldn't take a fortune of more than $500,000 for this by-product. A perfect and solidly reassuring example of the unpredictability of author-ego.

If further evidence is needed that Mario is a great human being, it might be found in his refusal to express anything but gratitude to Paramount from the very beginning for giving him a guarantee of only $50,000 for screen rights to *The Godfather*, and thus locking up the greatest bargain in movie history.

"That amount of money was the whole world to me, then," Mario said. "It was not only the most money I had ever had in one lump, but it was practically the first time I was ever out of debt. Paramount took a chance on me and it paid off for them. They don't owe me a thing."

It makes a nice ending for the story that Paramount came up with an additional payment, without being asked, of $100,000 for Mario's writing the screenplay, plus a piece of the picture's profits that is paying off big, possibly $1 million.

That account of Mario—the writing and selling of *The Godfather* and the novel's unexcelled success after the author's early failure to secure a publisher for it—is another example that authors, and those who hope to become authors, can draw support, comfort, and encouragement from. Indeed this pattern of dramatic success for a book rejected in its first submission is an all too familiar one that characterizes a business where chance, the tastes, judgments, and efforts of many others in addition to the author (including editors, film producers, publicity directors, booksellers, and reviewers) play vital, dramatic, and contributing parts.

The unexpected, the dramatic, and the unusual have always been part of publishing—as you will appreciate from reading the encouraging and discouraging experiences of authors whose personal efforts to help you become a writer, or to discard the idea entirely, make up the next portion of this book. You will find the contribution from John Toland is last, for no reason except that individual material from and about the authors is in alphabetical sequence.

ESCAPE
WITH A FLAIR
EDWARD S. AARONS

"Relentless . . . crisp . . . vigorous . . . harsh and credible," is what *The New York Times* says about the writing of Edward S. Aarons. The reviewer was commenting on No. 34 in the famous "Assignment" series, featuring handsome, smart Sam Durell, an intelligence agent physically able to take care of himself, with man or maiden. Sam is what is referred to in the trade as "a series hero," and the term pretty well explains itself with the information above that Ed Aarons has now published 39 books about the adventures of one Sam Durell in such romantic settings as Bangkok, Malta, Sumatra, Budapest, Sulu Sea, and other image-conjuring locations.

Ed didn't invent the series-character type of book but he has done very well with it as did Erle Stanley Gardner with Perry Mason, and John D. MacDonald does with Travis McGee, or Donald Hamilton with Matt Helm. An author is fortunate if he develops a hero the public wants to read more about. The big advantage of a series is that each new book finds readers who are encountering the series for the first time, and these readers become addicts who must read the books that have gone before. Thus, the series books are never out of print; they win themselves side-by-side displays on the paperback racks.

Ed calls his books "romantic adventure," and that is what they are; and they are also "escape reading," a very sure-fire commodity in the book business. Ed's books are titillating, not sexy, but they do concern men and women and adventure; and the reader is invited to go along, as per this cover blurb from *Assignment: Golden Girl*, "She called herself Sally, and her eyes were pure gold. The rest of her was a treasure too. And she wanted Sam to have it all."

If you are ever fortunate enough to develop a character your publisher wants to feature in a series, do so, and some day you may write to me in the same vein as Ed Aarons did: "I've found the rewards of writing to be so many that I count myself among the most fortunate of men. Aside from my personal 'life-style,' I feel the pleasure of knowing that so many readers are given a few hours of release and entertainment (I make no pretension for literary achievement) is extraordinarily gratifying. Fan mail from college faculty, students, business and professional men who read an 'Assignment' while flying on long trips and take the trouble to send their appreciation in a note, G.I.'s, even ministers, and once an old soldier in an old soldiers' home, give me more reward than I deserve."

Other rewards come his way, too, such as the royalty paid on the 23 million Sam Durell "Assignment Series" books in print.

The following are answers by author Aarons to questions you might have asked.

Q. What should a writer's discipline be?

A. As for the discipline under which writers work, it sums up to daily, regularly, unremittingly. If you truly love writing and want to achieve something in it, one can't idle around and wait for lightning in the form of "inspiration" to strike. None of the professionals I know idle about with that sort of thing. They work, as I try to do, every day, with regular hours, day in and day out. I've become so conditioned to this discipline that I feel subconsciously restless and uneasy and irritable if I am not working (as on a vacation), and something must always be "cooking on the back burner." The amount of time spent daily is difficult to define. I happen to be a morning worker, and put in three or four hours daily at the typewriter; but most often something is going on through all the waking hours, and small plot ideas, character images, etc., come at any time, when shaving, fishing, or sailing! The number of daily hours often depends on the fluidity of production, of course, but regularity at the typewriter is to me an essential ingredient of the discipline.

Q. What is your daily writing schedule?

A. Writing, while bringing ineffable satisfactions, is a solitary and secluded business. For example, I deliberately awake before my wife, quietly get my own breakfast (all the while considering the next scene, chapter, or plot problem) and go to the typewriter and ignore the telephone and visitors as much as possible. My own habits depend on my personal rhythms, of course. Everyone has varying energy rhythms of this sort. Some people are morning workers, others do best in the afternoons or evenings. A friend of mine, Clare Leighton, an Englishwoman who has done wonderful woodcuts and etchings of New England scenes for Wedgwood, refers to the difference by calling people "larks" who work in the morning, or the evening "nightingales."

Q. Where do you get story ideas?

A. The idea for novels comes from many sources—news, people, observed human situations. All one needs is the germ, the spark, the character that stimulates the writer to thinking about it. Incidentally, most ideas offered by well-meaning friends do not work, simply because the initial impulse must come from the writer and be his own creation, in order to provide the excitement and generate the stimulation to carry on through the long, hard weeks and months needed to reach completion. The idea grows and develops through characters, situations, and conflict most of all. Conflict should always be present, in the characters and the environment in which the characters are set.

Most of my ideas for "Assignment" books come from the news, but I must qualify that by the example of what happened after the very first "Assignment" book, *Assignment to Disaster*, appeared. The story dealt with the launching of the first U.S. space satellite, and was published only four days after Washington announced our Vanguard program. Twenty-four hours later I was visited by two neat young men (I still don't know if they were FBI or CIA) who wanted to know, very politely, how I'd gotten "classified information" on the Vanguard project, since obviously I'd had foreknowledge of the program. I gave them drinks and told them I got the idea from the newspapers. When they protested that nothing had appeared in the news on the program prior to the announcement four days before, I said, "Yes, but I read between the lines!" We shook hands and they left.

Q. How do you plan a novel?

A. To form the novel, so to speak, a rough outline or synopsis or list of "demand" scenes is worked out to develop the plot to crisis and denouement. But I find this outline does not become a rigid law unto itself. Let's call it a series of "guidelines." Very often, while writing, new ideas pop up, or a character may say something of his own volition that may radically alter the story's development.

95

These are, of course, the greatest and most satisfactory moments while writing. The outline, however, does help the writer proceed through the daily stints at the typewriter.

As for characters, nothing can be created in a total vacuum. For myself, as with most writers, I take a bit here and a piece there from real people, whether it be a mannerism, a habit of dress, a personality trait, etc. I've been shocked, sometimes, when people come up to me and say, "Hey, Ed, I see you put me in your story!" when in actual fact, I wasn't even thinking of them. To make the story mean something of course, the character must have within himself (or herself) some form of stress, conflict, striving, which must be satisfied or somehow resolved by the story's development. Writing a series character, of course, means for me that I have fun with this sort of thing in secondary characters also.

Q. What about research?

A. Research!!!! I treasure a onetime *New York Times* review which referred to me as his "favorite travelogue adventure writer." (Anthony Boucher.) I did much more traveling than I do now, having visited most of the places and backgrounds I've used, and my favorite means is by freighter, trains abroad, buses, anything but a tour. Most of this provides only the atmosphere, or mood, of a place. Back home, research digs out further details, maps, flora and fauna, and historical background. I find, for example, when walking down the street of some city abroad, most passersby can't identify flowers, trees, or historical figures offhand. So homework is vital. And often the research then affects the trend of the projected story, when something "exotic" or interesting is unearthed.

You may have noted that almost all of the "Assignment" books contain, somewhere, historical references to the environment.

I feel that none of us lives entirely in the present. The past is always an influence. My personal infatuation with ancient history becomes obvious, I think, in some of my books. (Have an M.A. in it, after a bachelor's degree in literature.) The problem is to slide in the background, so to speak, without slowing up the story's development! But for me, precedent lends weight and meaning to whatever you are writing about.

Q. Have you been influenced by other writers?

A. I admit briefly to an early devotion to Hemingway's novels (I spend my winters in Key West), and when I began on mystery-adventures, I read Dashiell Hammett avidly, who broke ground for today's realism. My personal reading today is still history and biography, however, with an occasional bow to the works of my competitors!

Q. Do you rewrite much?
A. As for rewriting: I do a rough draft, revise and cut once, then do a clean final copy while making further revisions of wordage while I go along.

Q. What started you on writing?
A. What pushed me into writing, I believe, was a background of a literate family, and I can always remember being surrounded by books in every room of the house. Have been a reader, most avid, since childhood. While in college, I began doing brief feature articles for the local newspapers, worked as a legman for almost two years, and then, wanting to be free of the rat race and the time clock, I started free-lancing short stories and novelettes for the magazines, beginning in the old pulps of the forties and achieving an occasional sale to the "slicks"—*Collier's, American Magazine,* and others. I sold and published my first novel just in time for my 21st birthday (and was paid $150.00 for it!) The main circumstance that made me become a writer, I think, was the desire to be myself and achieve what is now called a "life-style" that suited me—a need to avoid the sterility of today's digital, anonymous occupations. Writing, I may add, offers one of the very few occupations to achieve this sort of thing in today's technology and culture!

Q. What are your background experiences?
A. I attended the University of Pennsylvania, enlisted in the Navy two weeks after Pearl Harbor (had to finish a short story first, that I was working on!) and received my degrees afterward in New York at Columbia University. In between, as a teen-ager in the tail end of the Depression years, I worked in factories, drove a truck, was a salesman, sold hats through the Plains states and the West. Lived in New York, Boston, and Washington, D.C. Put in four years in the Navy in World War II, married a wonderful girl in 1946, risked everything on a tiny house in the wooded Connecticut hills, and went at writing. My wife and I went abroad almost every year from 1947 thereafter, on penny-pinching trips that were great fun and ultimately extraordinarily rewarding. I still live mainly in Connecticut, but the house is bigger, and I'm tired of shoveling snow, and a trick back forbids the enjoyment of toboggans, iceboats, and skiing, so the winters are mostly spent in Key West and West Indies islands.

The book titles that follow are those books of Mr. Aaron's authorship published by Fawcett Publications and do not necessarily represent all the books of his authorship. (The same is true of titles listed for other authors in this book unless otherwise stated.) Mr. Aarons writes other than Assignment books. The last four titles are not in that series.

Assignment Amazon Queen ● *Assignment Angelina* ● *Assignment Bangkok* ● *Assignment Black Viking* ● *Assignment Budapest* ● *Assignment Ceylon* ● *Assignment Cong Hai Kill* ● *Assignment: Golden Girl* ● *Assignment Karachi* ● *Assignment—Lowlands* ● *Assignment Maltese Maiden* ● *Assignment Moon Girl* ● *Assignment Nuclear Nude*● *Assignment: School for Spies* ● *Assignment—Silver Scorpion* ● *Assignment: Star Stealers* ● *Assignment Stella Marni* ● *Assignment Sulu Sea* ● *Assignment Sumatra* ● *Assignment Treason* ● *Assignment—White Rajah* ● *Don't Cry Beloved* ● *Escape to Love* ● *I Can't Stop Running* ● *State Department Murders* ●

A VERY VERSATILE MAN
ISAAC ASIMOV

Here is a man so widely superior in his scholarship and so prolific in his writings, I was tempted to leave him out of this manual of encouragement for fear a recital of his accomplishments would discourage anyone tempted to try writing.

Don't let his multiple attainments intimidate you. He is human, too, and a very likable human, with a great sense of humor, and there is much in his career that should interest you.

For one thing Isaac, who started as a fiction writer, has found himself almost deserting fiction and writing factual books on dozens of topics instead. Although I have not put much emphasis on nonfiction writing, it is a fact that more and more nonfiction books—books of a topical nature and interest—are being written. Not every one who contemplates writing as a career need be a fiction writer, although I believe the first dream of those who want to become writers is usually to write a novel. An experienced newspaper reporter or teacher could, if he would, astound himself by writing a successful nonfiction book on a subject that interests him. And so could many others.

Isaac has published, as of last week, 178 books. He sold his first science fiction at age eighteen, but has gone on to write about such varied subjects as Shakespeare, the slide rule, physics, algebra, American history, the Bible, humor, and book No. 177 is a second volume of "dirty" limericks of his own authorship, while No. 178 is a collection of his mystery short stories. Obviously Isaac feels competent to do a book on any subject that interests him, and you might just be able to do the same; although his interests and industry might be superior to yours. Maybe you don't want to write 178 books in 26-odd years.

It may help you feel superior to learn that although Isaac is one of the world's most famous science fiction writers he refuses to fly in an airplane. "Just scared," he says.

Isaac came to this country from Russia when very young, with his mother, father, and sister. His father worked for a time in the garment industry, but aspired to be his own boss and bought a small candy-newspaper-magazine store. This store was open to the public from 6:00 A.M. to midnight—often with Isaac helping out. Here it was that he became the voracious reader he is, reading particularly all the science fiction magazines that crowded the shelves. It was in these years, too, that he obtained his first library card and began to read without guidance through history, science, and literature. Each new subject built and complemented the others and it was then that his teachers discovered, and so did he, that he remembers almost everything he has ever read, an enormous help in research.

It is easy to call Isaac a genius, and he has been called that. School was absurdly easy for him. He skipped two grades—commonly read the textbooks intended for a semester in a single sitting. At an early age, he taught himself how to multiply in one evening, when he was skipped into a higher grade where multiplication had already been taught. And just so he would have them as handy reference, he learned the multiplication tables in one sitting.

Throughout the history of his unusual accomplishments there is a refreshing "directness" to everything Isaac has done; and I wonder if early in life he did not fashion his existence to that directness so logically that the accomplishments so often associated with "genius" just followed as a natural result. "The only thing to do!" Isaac might say, "and the only way to do it!"

Isaac never seems stumped on how to proceed. He just takes the direct way whether it is the writing of a book on Shakespeare, a biblical dissertation, or a science fiction novel. An example of this trait occurred when he was eighteen years old and was a total fan of a magazine, *Astounding Science Fiction*. When the June 1938 edition did not reach the newsstand on May 1, as was its custom, he went into a decline. Finally, on May 17, he took the subway from his home in the Bronx to 79 7th Avenue in Manhattan, where the publisher

(Street and Smith) was located in an imposing block-long building, to find out, simply and directly, why his favorite magazine was not on sale. There the young man sought out an official of the large publishing house and the official put Isaac's fear to rest with the information that the magazine had changed its publication date and that it would be on sale May 19.

Isaac was not surprised that the information he desired was obtained in such a fashion, or from such a source, and it followed just as naturally that when he had completed his first science fiction story that same year, he should again get on the subway and take the manuscript by hand to the editor of his favorite magazine, *Astounding Science Fiction*.

The editor was John Campbell and he saw and talked with the aspiring writer for an hour, recognizing from Isaac's enthusiasm and recall of stories read (their authors and which issues their stories were in) that here was a sincere reader and fan, if not an author. The first story of Isaac's was not accepted and was never published, but Campbell did work with the young man and the second story he wrote was accepted by another magazine after Campbell had rejected it as not good enough for *Astounding*—then the best of the science fiction magazines. Subsequently Campbell bought many of Isaac's stories.

Certainly editor Campbell, with his courtesy and interest in the eager young man, gave the kind of encouragement and help that shaped the career of one who went on to become one of our most famous popular writers. Would Asimov have persevered to become a writer without such a personal stimulus from editor Campbell? Probably. It is hard to imagine anything deterring Isaac, but the "hand up" was gratifying, most encouraging, and possibly more important than can be proven.

Many years later Isaac asked John Campbell, by then a close friend and valued editor, why he had taken time to talk to him at all, since the first story he handed him, called "Cosmic Corkscrew," was so bad that it had never been accepted or published anywhere.

"It was utterly impossible," Campbell agreed. "On the other hand, I saw something in *you*. You were eager and you listened and I knew you wouldn't quit no matter how many rejections I handed you. As long as you were willing to work hard at improving, I was willing to work with you."

And, for your information, that statement holds for every professional editor once he recognizes that the would-be author is worth working with. I'm afraid though you will have difficulty today walking into a large book publishing house, manuscript in hand, and spending an hour with a helpful editor.

For the first thirteen years of his writing career, Isaac wrote only science fiction short stories. He is one of many authors who became writers of books after serving an apprenticeship in writing for the pulp magazines that existed in such numbers in the 1930s. There is no doubt that these magazines served as a school for beginning writers of that day. There was a great variety of subject matter in these pulp magazines, including mysteries, detective stories, science fiction, westerns, battle stories, love stories, and adventures of all kinds, but whether it was a natural and good school to produce novelists is debatable. Certainly only a very few of the literally thousands of contributors to these magazines went on to be novelists.

For one thing the payments were so low, both for magazine story writing and novel writing in that era that really able people went into other occupations. No doubt had the rewards been larger for book writing, many of those who wrote then for magazines would have written books.

By the time Isaac was 29, he had taken three degrees from Columbia University, including a Ph.D. in chemistry, and during those years he had published 60 short stories, out of which his total earnings had come to $7,821.75, averaging a little over $710 per year. In his better years he had earned $1,600 and in the 10th and 11th years together he had earned only $3,300.

That's why, in 1949, after getting his Ph.D. he had to find a job. He first turned down, and then accepted, a job in the Biochemistry Department of Boston University School of Medicine for $5,000 annually.

He soon became Associate Professor of Biochemistry and wrote a textbook for medical students called *Biochemistry and Human Metabolism*, in collaboration with Professors Walker and Boyd.

It was in this period that he wrote his first book-length tale, a science fiction work, *Pebble in the Sky*. It happened as a result of his meeting Doubleday editor Walter I. Bradbury at a gathering of science fiction authors. Walter had been attracted to Isaac through reading a science fiction magazine serial Isaac had written, and suggested he try a book.

Isaac says of this offer: "I paid little attention to this proposal. The thought of publishing a book, as opposed to magazine stories, was so outlandish that I simply couldn't cram it into my head."

Isaac told Fred Pohl, a friend who was also an agent, of Bradbury's interest, and it was Pohl who suggested Isaac show Bradbury a rejected short story, *Grow Old With Me*, as the possible basis for a science fiction novel. (See how agents can help?)

Bradbury read the story, was interested in the theme as a basis for a novel, and paid Isaac the first option money he ever got, $250, which he could keep if the rewrite was unsatisfactory. On April 6, 1949, he began the revision and on May 25, 1949, it was finished and retitled *Pebble in the Sky*. On May 29, Doubleday accepted it, but the payment was so small Isaac had to take the Boston job, although he did not want to leave New York and the people he knew in publishing.

By 1952 he was making more money as an author than he was as a professor, and the discrepancy grew larger—in favor of writing —each succeeding year. By 1957 he decided that he would become a full-time author and on July 1, 1958, gave up his salary and duties but with the agreement of Boston University, kept his title of Associate Professor of Biochemistry. He still gives an occasional lecture at the school.

"Writing is easy now," Isaac says, "and is even more satisfying. I keep what amounts to a seventy-hour week, if you count all the ancillary jobs of proofreading, indexing, research, and so on. In the past six years, I have averaged a book a month.

"Still, I must admit there has never been, since 1949, anything like the real excitement of those first eleven years and my association with John Campbell, when I wrote only in my spare time, when every submission meant unbearable suspense, when every rejection meant misery and every acceptance ecstasy, and every fifty-dollar check was the wealth of Croesus."

When I told Isaac of my project to encourage people to become authors, the same mind that had sent him to find out from an executive of Street and Smith why his favorite magazine was not on sale when due gave out this spontaneous response: "They should write. Everyone who wants to should write."

When I asked about his work habits, I got the following:

"I'm not sure if my work habits should be imitated. I don't have set hours for working. I just write whenever I feel like, but I feel like it all the time. Where social and biological urges and duties are not involved, I write all the time. I am always engaged in a large number of different writing tasks so that I switch from one to the other as the mood hits me, and in this way I have managed to avoid a writing block over a period of thirty-four years.

"I work on the typewriter, typing ninety words a minute, and do as little rewriting as I can. I do some, of course, usually in pen and ink directly on the first draft. Then I retype it and that's it.

"I do very little research, because I have been reading avidly all my life and remember virtually everything I read. To back me up, however, I have developed a personal reference library in my office of some two thousand books or so in all fields.

"As to my fiction specifically—I think up an ending; then I decide on a beginning; then get to work. I make it up as I go along, keeping a chapter ahead of myself more or less and aiming always at that decided-upon ending."

I might interject here that Isaac's procedure of working out a novel's ending first can be done in science fiction because of the author's involvement with scientific theory and goals. It would be rare that another kind of novel could be developed in that fashion.

Isaac says this about training for authorship: "I have never had any training in writing. I have never had any writing courses in school. I have never read books on it. I have never asked advice (except for that which is given me spontaneously by my editors). As far as I know, I write purely instinctively, and how anyone can learn to do that, I haven't the faintest idea.

"The big thing is that I enjoy the actual mechanics of writing. I love to peck out the words on my typewriter (I use the touch system); I don't suffer; I don't agonize. I don't have to drive myself. I just write."

There, have you got it? Don't suffer, don't agonize, don't drive yourself, just write: possibly, only if your name is Isaac Asimov.

If you want to know more about this remarkable man—his writing, his experiences—see his books *The Early Asimov*, Books I and II, as published in Fawcett paperbacks.

Here are other books by Asimov.

Before the Golden Age, Books I and II ● *The Caves of Steel* ● *The Currents of Space* ● *The Early Asimov, Book I* ● *The Early Asimov, Book II* ● *Earth Is Room Enough* ● *The End of Eternity* ● *The Gods Themselves* ● *The Hugo Winners (Vol. I)* ● *I, Robot* ● *The Martian Way* ● *More Stories from the Hugo Winners, Vol. II* ● *The Naked Sun* ● *Nightfall and Other Stories* ● *Nine Tomorrows* ● *Pebble in the Sky* ● *The Stars, Like Dust* ● *Stories from the Hugo Winners, Vol. II* ● *Where Do We Go From Here?* ● *An Easy Introduction to the Slide Rule* ● *Realm of Algebra* ● *Realm of Numbers* ●

A WRITER AND A SCHOLAR
SAUL BELLOW

With only eight novels this man has captured the literary world and the critics to a degree unequaled by any other writer of this generation. So impressive are his awards, topped by the Nobel Prize for

Literature in 1976, that they are worth listing, at least in part: *Humboldt's Gift* won the Pulitzer Prize for Fiction in 1976; *The Adventures of Augie March* won the National Book Award for Fiction in 1954; *Herzog* won the same award in 1965; *Mr. Sammler's Planet* won it in 1971. *Herzog* also was awarded the International Literary Prize, and Mr. Bellow became the first American to win this award in the five years the awards have been established. In 1968 the Republic of France awarded him the Croix de Chevalier des Arts et Lettres, the highest literary distinction awarded by that nation to noncitizens, and in the same year he received the B'nai B'rith Jewish Heritage Award for "excellence in Jewish literature." He was the recipient of the Friends of Literature Award in 1960, the James L. Dow Award in 1964, and the French Prix International de Literature in 1965.

Saul Bellow is professor, Committee on Social Thought at the University of Chicago, and has a list of academic credits longer than that of his literary awards. In response to my suggestion that he might contribute some information or suggestions for this book, he supplied four short statements, each pertinent. The first one should be read over slowly several times, probably aloud.

It is this:	"My first book was accepted for publication. When I read the manuscript through I decided to destroy it. I then wrote *Dangling Man* in 1942. Dial Press turned it down. Vanguard accepted it."
The second:	"I was a bookish and sickly child."
The third:	"My writing day is five or six hours."
The fourth:	"To rewrite ten times is not unusual."

The following books by Saul Bellow have been published in paperback:

The Adventures of Augie March. ●● *Henderson the Rain King.* ● *Herzog* ● *Mr. Sammler's Planet* ● *Seize the Day* ● *Mosby's Memoirs and Other Stories* ●

A VERY FUNNY PEG
PEG BRACKEN

Oh, life has trials which bruise and blister, and
*   which*
Can sear the soul, but this one is the worst:
To start the second half of any sandwich
And find that all your meat was in the first.
                            —*P. BRACKEN*

That poem proves Peg Bracken is what the world needs most—a funny writer. She is not only a funny writer, she writes funny. She talks funny. She is funny and she is a great deal of fun to be with. Funny things happen when Peg is around. But she is not funny to look at. She is a very attractive lady.

Actually she started being funny on the side, since her real job at the time was that of copywriter for a Cleveland, Ohio, department store, and there isn't room for a great deal of funny stuff when you are writing ads whose purpose is to sell something like women's underwear, or pots and pans, or whatever. "Funny on the side," means she wrote some whimsical poetry for *Good Housekeeping* and some essays for *The New Yorker* while working as a copywriter. This writing on the side led to a nationally syndicated funny essay column three days a week. "And writing a funny column three days a week isn't funny," she is supposed to have said, but her column was funny, very funny and very popular. In fact, she got so rich being funny three days a week in her column she was able to retire to a life of rural interests and tennis and writes only enough to turn out a book every several years. In between, though, she fills a lot of speaking engagements, writes a monthly column for *Family Circle* magazine, does some commercials on TV, and says funny things to her friends.

Peg's first book was *The I Hate to Cook Book*, a tremendous seller in both hardcover and paperback, followed by more fun of the same kind called *Appendix to the I Hate to Cook Book*, *I Didn't Come Here to Argue*, followed recently by an account of her travels in Europe, *But I Wouldn't Have Missed It for the World*, and in 1976 *The I Hate to Cook Almanack: A Book of Days*.

It is difficult enough to be a successful writer, but it is more than twice as hard to be a successful funny writer. Everyone wants to laugh, but "everyone" does not laugh at the same things or for the same reasons—or for the same reasons two days in a row.

If you want to write funny, do so. Don't be any more discouraged than you have to and keep on trying just like a normal human writer. The rewards are great if you can make people laugh, both in money and in just listening.

Here is Peg, herself, for your enlightenment:

I think writing is hard, almost too hard. Yet writing is a joyous activity when it is going well.

The big trouble is, no matter what he is writing, the writer's job is to create a world in which the reader unconsciously suspends judgment and accepts—at least momentarily—the author's implicit assumption that it matters whether the hero gets the girl or the anti-hero gets the boy, or this frog jumps farther than that frog, or whether the monarchy stands or falls, or ditto the soufflé. Creating any world isn't easy.

I wish, as most writers do, that one could install a dependable hot line to the unconscious. It is a homely comparison, but the writing process reminds me of my vacuum cleaner, which is a compact type with an accessory attachment named, somewhat lyrically, the Power Wand. Perhaps the sales manager christened it for the spring sales meeting, or more probably his wife did after she tried it, for it certainly cleans. The Power Wand contains its own motor, so that when it is plugged into the cleaner itself, which has a motor too, the power is doubled. Then it picks up everything in sight, including things you didn't know were there.

Writing seems to me to be that way on one's good days. A power wand is operating. But on other days, unfortunately, the writer can't think where in the world he put it last time.

I think this is partly what Brancusi meant when he said: "To do it, yes, easy, but to arrive at the state of mind in which one can do it—that is another matter." Writing regularly tends to make that power wand, or auxiliary resource, more readily available. Even so, it is rather will-o'-the-wisp.

Freud wrote somewhere that he worked best in a condition of moderate misery. I find that to be true. A slight malaise—physical, mental, or emotional—is helpful; for writing is essentially a curative process, I believe, but there must be something to cure. Rude health and euphoria are handicaps; there is no need to write then. Perhaps many writers know this unconsciously and—equally unconsciously but to good purpose—drink too much or complicate their sex lives or otherwise give themselves something to write their way out of. But there is no real need to be so drastic: a glance at the morning headlines should be sufficient.

I would like to try to write two or three books at once, though I

106

haven't yet. Many painters have several paintings in work simultaneously—all different—so that the fallout from one gives fresh direction to another. If the books were varied enough, it should be an ideal solution, or at least ameliorate another of the writer's problems—what to do when he isn't writing.

Early in the morning is my writing time, from four or five A.M. till around noon. It is true that the first hour or so is a sleepy part of the day. I've learned by now that the brain wakes up one chunk at a time, and I take it as a matter of course that I won't shift out of neutral till I've been at it for an hour or so. But these hours are still far better for me than later in the day, when the fuzz is off the peach.

When I wake up with a taut feeling in the pit of my stomach, it augurs well for a good working day. I think it is interesting how the viscera seem to be involved in any act of grace or courage, and it seems to me that writing requires both; courage, because any writing is self-revelatory. We don't see the world as it is but the way we are, and this comes through.

But sometimes the visceral signals are wrong; sometimes it was only something I ate. If so, I work bleakly, with a sense of total incompetence. I ask myself (to no avail) how So-and-so would handle this problem, this paragraph; and it occasionally helps then to remember Rabbi Golden's reflection on one of his down days . . . "God will never ask me why I was not Moses, but He will ask me why I was not Rabbi Golden."

At times like this, I find the mechanics of writing especially troublesome, though fortunately distracting as well. I mean those thorny words that don't sound like what they mean or have a subtly wrong coloration, and the pronoun that stubbornly refers to the wrong antecedent, and the sentences that limp home dangling their participles behind them, and all the other assorted booby traps that dot the meadow. I feel warm kinship with the writer who wrote, "That morning in the yard, he saw two mongooses." It sounded poor, so he rewrote it: "That morning in the yard, he saw two mongeese." Which still left something to be desired, and so he tried once again: "That morning in the yard, he saw a mongoose. Almost immediately then, he saw another mongoose. . . ."

About organization: I am no good at it. I write from a general idea, or ghost of an idea, never being sure where it is going to go. With me, the words create the thought far more often than the other way around.

I wish it were otherwise and that I could cleave to a written outline, but when I make myself do that, the thing goes flat. This is a handicap. I think it was Maugham who said that few writers write as they would like to, only as best they can, and that despite himself the writer makes his limitations the cornerstone of his craft.

I do a great deal of rewriting. Almost never is a paragraph right the first time or the sixth or seventh time either. "Don't sweat the little things" doesn't apply to humor (or whatever it is that I write; the term isn't exact though I suppose it comes as close as any). I must sweat the little things because they are my only medium: small black words, like a musician's small black notes, the right ones in the right order. There is a grave difference between a B and a B flat, and it matters too where it falls in the measure.

I believe there is only one best word, even if it is a micrometric decision, for any purpose. Of course one doesn't always find that best word, but it is the thing to aim for. If, in a sentence, another word can be substituted, or the order of the words altered, and no harm done, it couldn't have been a very good sentence to begin with.

I don't think I'm alone in this; and I believe it is disconcerting to most writers when an incompetent editor changes a word or a sentence merely to flex his muscles or for the joy of changing. The writer doesn't want to see the editor fired, necessarily, just neatly drawn and quartered and fed to the crocodiles.

On the other hand, when a sensitive and intelligent editor miraculously improves upon what the writer considered perfection, it is a boon and a blessing. Fatuousness can cloud one's judgment of one's own child; a parent can't always see that his child's teeth need straightening, but he is usually glad to have the fact pointed out by someone who knows. With the professional writer, it is the quality of the finished work that counts.

Even matters of punctuation loom large. At best it is a scant and clumsy selection of punctuation marks that the writer has at his disposal. When he has carefully considered the alternatives before finally choosing from what's available, he generally wants it to remain that way. Robert Louis Stevenson's rage was controlled but evident in the note he once sent back with his galley proofs: "If I receive another proof of this sort, I shall return it at once with the general direction 'See Mr. S.' I must suppose my system of punctuation to be very bad; but it is mine; and it shall be adhered to with punctual exactness by any created printer who shall print for me."

I can't remember a time when I didn't write, or want to write. When I was six or seven years old, I loved office equipment stores and stationery shops—paper, carbon paper, paper clips, blank books, staplers. They held a magic for me that other shops didn't. I still feel that way.

Somewhere I read that if you enjoy the pedestrian details of your work—cleaning up after it, caring for your equipment, and so on—it is probably the right work for you. By that criterion I am in the right job. I like to type, file, lick stamps, change typewriter ribbons; and few activities beat the pleasure of making a fair copy of a much-chewed page.

In paperback by Peg Bracken:
Appendix to the I Hate to Cook Book ● But I Wouldn't Have Missed It for the World ● The I Hate to Cook Book ● The I Hate to Housekeep Book ● I Didn't Come Here to Argue ● I Try to Behave Myself ● The I Hate to Cook Almanack: A Book of Days ●

IN A CLASS BY HERSELF
TAYLOR CALDWELL

If you are among the thousands who greet each new Taylor Caldwell novel with cheers of welcome, you should treat yourself and read a small book about her, and written by her, entitled *On Growing up Tough.* This is the closest thing to an autobiography, or biography, of the lady who was given the imposing string of names, Janet Miriam Taylor Holland Caldwell, when she was born in Manchester, England, where her father was a staff artist of the *Manchester Guardian,* one of the world's outstanding newspapers.

This little book is a collection of short magazine pieces she has been persuaded to write about herself, her background, her philosophy, and her opinions.

On Growing up Tough is an accurate description of her early years and her later years. Taylor Caldwell is still growing up tough, and she is tough today. Hers was a background that either tempers and strengthens the person who lives it, as hammer blows temper sword steel, or breaks it. She didn't break.

A would-be burglar-assailant can testify to that. She surprised the intruder while descending the stairs from the second floor of her Buffalo, New York, home a few years ago. He ran toward her, up the stairs, and she took off through the upstairs bedrooms, slamming doors behind her, and finally securing herself in a room whose only door had a chain latch, which permitted the door to open only a few inches. When the burglar stuck his hand through in an effort to slip the chain, Janet Miriam Taylor Holland Caldwell sank her teeth into the fleshy upper joint of the man's thumb and bit until her teeth hit bone.

Her opinions are as strong as her bite, her hates as strong as her loves. High on the hate list are communists, spoiled youth, hippies, people willing to live on handouts, "liberals," unmanly men, and plastic anythings. High on her love list are manly men, real democracy, honesty in government, hard work for self and fellow man, her religion (Catholic), real wool yarn, honest combed cotton, hand-tooled wood, and 100-proof bourbon.

Taylor looks back with appreciation that her mother took her out of school at fifteen and sent her job hunting. She found heavy laboring work in a factory, six days a week, twelve hours a day.

Her first schooling was in England at Miss Brother's School, her age four. By the time she was seven she had two years of Latin and one of French and was "reading Shakespeare's sonnets, England's minor poets, and had a good grounding in history and geography. No guidance counselors, no twittering on the part of teachers, no soft patting hands, no cherishing. We were being prepared for life," she states.

She says of this early life, after her middle-class British parents brought her to America, where her father became staff artist at Niagara Lithograph Co., Buffalo, New York: "My parents, as much as they could, carried on the Spartan life for me, in spite of the softness they saw all around us in America for pampered children. I was earning my spending money when I was seven, after I finished my schoolwork and my chores at home. Saturdays and Sundays were tough days—ironing, mending, darning, snow shoveling, grass cutting, glass polishing, homework, Sunday school, and church twice a day.

"When I was ten I was working at the local market on Saturday filling up bags and helping wait on customers. I looked all of fifteen.

"When I was fifteen, after the factory episode, I held a full-time job as secretary. (I had paid for my own tuition at the Hurst Business School.) After work I went to night high school. Sunday was my free day. I had a Sunday school class of my own, then hurried home to help with dinner, prepare my clothing for the next day, and do my school homework. I was up at half-past five on Monday to get my father's breakfast plus mine and my brother's, and on my way to work by six-forty. Not much time for loitering and 'alienation.' "

She married early, was a mother of a year-old-child at nineteen, and spent two years with her construction-engineer husband living in tents and abandoned log cabins in Kentucky while he engaged in a fruitless search for oil and fortune. For most of that time they were forty miles from a railroad. She and her baby were brought in to join her husband by a mule-pulled wagon, a two-day trip. "I learned to grow vegetables," she says of that early life. "I had a corn patch, a

110

patch of lettuce and carrots, radishes and potatoes. Once a week I gathered up my baby and walked five miles to Benton, the nearest village, over mountains, across pastures and streams, to buy staples such as coffee, sugar, and salt. I made my own bread on a kerosene stove. I cured my own bacon and ham in the smokehouse my husband built."

There it was the mountain women taught her to sew and knit and even to weave blankets from wool, to make all her family's clothing, to gather herbs for medicine, how to deliver babies.

After two years of this backwoods living, her husband's oil endeavors took them to Bowling Green, Kentucky, and after several years more his employer went broke, and the young husband could not collect his back salary. All the money they had was fifty dollars Taylor had saved from six months' work as a public stenographer.

The decision was made to move back to Buffalo. Taylor was to go first with the baby, the husband to follow; after two days and a night in a railroad coach she arrived at 6:30 A.M. in Buffalo, New York, in the midst of a February blizzard and below zero weather. The Salvation Army helped her find a rooming house and a job as secretary to a kindly Mr. Lester Schweitzer at $25 weekly. A few months later he insisted on loaning her his only office typewriter so that she might compete for a job as a court reporter, which she qualified for. From court reporter she went, shortly, as secretary to the Department of Justice in Buffalo.

It was then, when she was a twenty-year-old, hard-working, full-time secretary, that Taylor Caldwell began writing seriously in a determined effort to become a published author of novels. She had enjoyed writing since her early school days, essays, poems, short stories, and even an attempt at a full-length novel when she was twelve.

And not until eighteen years later, when she was thirty-eight years old, did she have the thrill of holding the first published novel of her authorship in hand. The book: *Dynasty of Death*. It was an instant best-seller.

In those eighteen years, from the time she made up her mind to become an author to the day she had a novel published, Taylor Caldwell wrote a total of seven novels. Six of them were rejected by various publishers until *Dynasty of Death* was published to great success.

Following that success the earlier written novels were published to enthusiastic reader appreciation and large sales in both hard-cover and paperback editions.

This experience in attempting unsuccessfully to market novels over nearly a twenty-year period, novels that eventually became

111

best-sellers, is a chilling one and possibly typical of the industry's attitude toward would-be authors in an earlier time.

"I spent every penny I could save out of a tiny salary to send my novels to publishers," Taylor Caldwell says with a wry, nostalgic grimace, "but none were accepted until *Dynasty of Death*.

"There was rarely any evidence my submitted manuscripts had been read, and frequently the precious stamps I enclosed for return postage for the manuscripts were confiscated by someone in the publishing house and the manuscript returned to me, collect, via Railway Express.

"In those days the purloined stamps represented big money to me and meant skimping on food or delaying purchase of needed clothing."

Such unflagging determination in the instances of rejection after rejection, year after year, could only be maintained by one whose confidence and talent could not be denied. The manuscripts were sent to a large selection of publishers, addressed to the firm, not to the name of any individual editor.

I do believe had the submissions been addressed to an editor in one of the leading publishers of that day she would have been published much earlier. I am saddened and feel more than a small shame for the industry, that some perceptive person did not sample his or her publisher's slush pile and rescue one of those early manuscripts that has now gone on to be a best-seller so belatedly. Saddened, too, that some ambitious young editor didn't make his own fame by finding gold in the slush.

In today's market, with publishers competing so avidly for publishable manuscripts, I would like to believe her experience could not be duplicated. However, to be on the safe side, do not fail to address your manuscript to an individual in the publishing house of your choice.

Taylor Caldwell on the stand:

Q. Do you swear to tell the truth, nothing but, etc. etc.?
A. I do.

Q. What advice would you give anyone who desires to become an author?
A. If you are really meant to be a writer, I think you will write and write and write, and keep on writing. There is no obstacle strong enough to keep you from writing except, possibly, for short periods. You will go back to it.

Q. Can you suggest a writing regimen?

A. Only for myself. I used to write whenever I could steal a moment or an hour. Now I write at night, from about midnight until dawn. Nights are far more beautiful than days, and I feel "alive" at night. I'm a night person. Moreover, there are no interruptions at night—no telephones, no doorbells. I avoid these by sleeping during the day. It is too bad—in my opinion—that nights are so short and days are so long. It should be just the reverse! That is why I prefer winter to summer. But I do cultivate a garden in summer—after the sun goes down and the dark descends. With a flashlight.

Q. Do you write every night?

A. When I'm lucky I do, but my writing habits are erratic. I don't belong to the school of "one thousand words before breakfast, two thousand words between breakfast and lunch, and two thousand words to five o'clock." That is too mechanistic. When I start to write I do not stop until I have completely exhausted what I had in mind for that night. Then I have to wait until another idea occurs to me from out of my subconscious. Sometimes that idea comes within four or five hours, and sometimes not for four or five weeks; and one time I had to put aside a book for three years before the "well" filled up again.

Q. What about research?

A. When I am planning a book, I do elaborate research, sometimes traveling abroad to the Vatican and elsewhere. I am constantly traveling for local color, etc., all over the world.

Q. Much rewriting?

A. Indeed. After writing about twenty pages, I go over them and over them and over them, cutting and changing words to bring out the meaning more clearly. Sometimes I destroy the pages entirely. Or, at best, I rewrite them several times. When a manuscript is sent to the editor it may be copiously marked up, cut and corrected, but it is readable and ready for the printer. It is the best I can do. I never do anything but my best, and if I think what I have done is not my best it never sees my editor's eyes.

Q. Do you put aside your writing for other things?

A. Not if I am working on a book. It is my belief a novelist should not permit family crises, or health, or worries of any kind, to interfere with his work. If I had stopped to let family disasters, even deaths in the family, have their prolonged place in my life I should never have been able to turn out the large body of work I have done. Nor have I ever failed a deadline, no matter the upheaval in my affairs and catastrophies of major proportions. I turned out two of my best books during a five-year endless disaster which grew worse

113

every day. Businessmen, doctors, and lawyers have to keep some kind of schedule and so should writers.

Q. Do you read your books after they are published?
A. Only after a considerable time has passed. Then I read and reread the books I have written to see where I could have improved them, where I could have cut, where I could have introduced another line of thought, where they could have been sharpened. This helps in future writing. It can also encourage or discourage.

Q. Is writing a pleasure for you?
A. When it goes well, the level of pleasure is very high and very satisfying. In some instances the experience verges on the supernatural, when the characters in the book take over and speak their lines with no conscious thought on my part. My fingers fly on the typewriter keys and I have no awareness of forming sentences. It is as if some exterior force is controlling me and I am an observer as the words jump onto the paper like a magic trick.

When this happens, and it does frequently, I write until I am exhausted. When I don't reread until the next day, it is as though someone else has written it; I have only the faintest memory of having seen the words before. Sometimes no memory.

The following books by Taylor Caldwell are in paperback:
The Arm and the Darkness ● *Captains and the Kings* ● *Dialogues With the Devil* ● *The Final Hour* ● *Glory and the Lightning* ● *Grandmother and the Priests* ● *Great Lion of God* ● *The Late Clara Beame* ● *Maggie, Her Marriage* ● *No One Hears but Him* ● *On Growing Up Tough* ● *A Pillar of Iron* ● *The Romance of Atlantis* ● *Testimony of Two Men* ● *To Look and Pass* ● *Wicked Angel* ●

I WOULD NEVER CONTEMPLATE ANY OTHER WAY OF LIFE
DOROTHY EDEN

Dorothy Eden lives in England in a charming old London square. She has written thirty-five books and admits to an ego glow because she is published in at least sixteen languages.

Born in rural New Zealand, she says of her first book: "The sale of my first novel was a traumatic experience. This was in the early days of the Second World War, when I was living in New Zealand. Communication with England was long, tedious, and hazardous. It took three months for a letter to arrive. However, I hopefully posted my manuscript and waited no less than a year, when at last the agent to whom I had sent it reported its nonarrival. It no doubt still reposes at the bottom of the ocean. But a second copy was sent, arrived safely, and was sold. This was a salutary lesson in patience, and I do think patience is one of the more important virtues of a writer."

Ms. Eden is well-known for her period and historical fiction, as well as her suspense and modern gothic novels; she does shy a bit at the term "gothic," as applied to her books, but the public insists on so-calling and buying them, so she accepts the term.

Like so many who have become authors, she admits to having always wanted to be a writer, and the fact that she did is still a surprise: "I cannot say what contributed to my becoming an author, except that it was simply always what I meant to be, in spite of enormous difficulties, a childhood on a remote New Zealand farm, and no connection whatever with the literary world.

"I was always a reader, and my early childhood was opened to the world of Grimm's fairy tales. I have always been influenced by authors, and I think the one who has made the most impression on me is Wilkie Collins and his *The Woman in White*.

"It would be a real pleasure to assist in your campaign to encourage authorship and in response to your questions I would say I do not spend a long working day as I suffer rather badly from arthritis, and indeed have a long year of operations ahead of me. But writing remains as always my escape and my therapy. As a writer one doesn't have to spend one's whole life being the same person—a great joy.

"In a further effort to be helpful I am enclosing some material I hope will be of use to you."

While the material she sent me is, as a whole, more concerned with the mechanics of writing than I am here, there are several very helpful parts that fit our purpose:

"A good story is always sought after and salable—important if you want to live by your work. And from the days of the *Arabian Nights* storytelling has been a compulsive art, both for the teller and listener alike. I do not think this is going to change, simply because human nature does not basically change.

"So I would advise would-be writers not to be too obsessed by gimmicks or fashions, above all not to slavishly copy a successful writer. Be yourself, create good strong characters, and open your mind to them. Above all, write about something with which you are familiar and can communicate.

"A writer is only a pen on paper, a manuscript, a voice through which his characters speak. But try to make it an individual voice."

The emphasis Ms. Eden puts on story characters, above, is a strong clue as to how she invents and plots a novel. So similar is her approach to that of many other writers of popular fiction I am going to include her comments on story construction and plot development, although it is verging on the kind of specific instruction I do not mean to characterize this book. Remember? I'm trying to encourage, not instruct. Here is Ms. Eden again:

"When I plot a story, I let things and images drop into my mind until a shadowy story forms. This is a lovely easy dreaming period that makes me keep postponing the real work, i.e., getting an outline on paper. When I finally get down to that, I am inclined to type out the outline several times, while it clarifies. I list possible incidents, I name my characters and make notes about their appearance, their nature, their motivation. They must appear vividly in my mind. If they don't they will eventually shrivel up and disappear.

"I always know how the story will end, although I never follow a rigid path toward that end; and when my characters are ready to do so, I allow my characters to take over their own scenes.

"When I say 'when they are ready to do so,' I mean this literally. There is always a period, sometimes brief, sometimes much too long, but always disheartening, when one's characters obstinately remain strangers and shadows. I struggle with them. I threaten to give them up and send them back into limbo. Sometimes this struggle goes on for one or two hundred pages. But I know that just as I won't let them go, they won't let me go. They lurk like ghostly images in the back of my mind, until suddenly in a scene, in a paragraph, even a sentence, they break through, come alive, and take over. From that point on my major troubles are over. I am willingly possessed.

"Names are most important to me, and sometimes by changing a name I see a character more clearly.

"As to the heroine in these romantic suspense novels, it is unfortunate that she must be rather vague and dreamy, almost, I'm sorry to say, stupid. Otherwise she would get to the bottom of the mysterious happenings by the third chapter.

"I consider all plots of the gothic novel farfetched, but the secret is in making the background so interesting and unusual, the action so vivid, and the characters so alive that the reader is swept along on an uncritical tide. Involvement is the word, for both reader and author. I can assure you that if the author has remained uninvolved, the reader will suffer from this very easily communicated disease and care little about what happens to Lucy or Sarah or whomever.

"I remain uninvolved, or only half involved, until my characters begin to talk to me. If this felicitous state of affairs doesn't happen, then I regretfully put my notes away in a drawer, perhaps forever, perhaps to be resurrected a year or two later, when the story may come to life.

"The long, partly historical novels I write are another matter entirely. I particularly like evoking a period and being able to dispense with the dreamy and rather too-pure heroine. I can select the kind of house suitable to the period and then have a marvelous time filling it with the kind of people whom I'm sure once lived there. In these novels happiness is not necessary in the ending, but there must be resolution. There must be a strong theme; it can be business, a lawsuit, family feuds. For me it is always a working out of human emotions over a long period, the progress of a marriage, or the growing up of a family.

"I can never see the final shape of this kind of book until it is nearly finished, and I go through phases of elation and despair as my characters tug me this way and that, frequently into avenues I had never imagined. But it is all constantly absorbing, and I would never contemplate any other way of life."

Following are those of Dorothy Eden's books in paperback:
An Afternoon Walk ● *Darkwater* ● *Lady of Mallow* ● *The Marriage Chest* ● *Melbury Square* ● *The Millionaire's Daughter* ● *Never Call It Loving* ● *Ravenscroft* ● *The Shadow Wife* ● *Siege in the Sun* ● *Sleep in the Woods* ● *Speak to Me of Love* ● *The Vines of Yarrabee* ● *Waiting for Willa* ● *Winterwood* ●

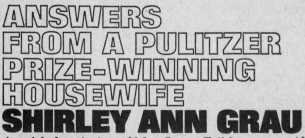

ANSWERS FROM A PULITZER PRIZE-WINNING HOUSEWIFE
SHIRLEY ANN GRAU

A quick description of Mrs. James Feiblemann—wife of the retired head of the Philosophy Department, Tulane University, and himself author of more than thirty books—would be: Shirley Ann Grau, housewife, Pulitzer Prize-winning mother of four children, and author of six serious novels and story collections in twenty years.

She is exceptionally frank and fast in answer to questions, and once greeted an interviewer from a newspaper at the front door of her home shortly after the second ring of the door chimes, joined by the barking of dogs.

"I'm sorry," she explained, "I had to secure the German shepherds. They're not exactly friendly. We got them for protection, and I've found it works too well. We've ended with protection from everybody. I mean the man who reads the gas meter, delivery boys, the postman. Why he—the postman—won't even come up the driveway anymore. He just leaves packages and hollers for someone to pick them up. Thankfully, the dogs get along very well with the children. The dogs are afraid of the children," she added with a grin.

This remarkable lady, who commonly takes a year and a half, or more, to mull over an idea for a novel before actually writing anything of it, has such interesting answers that I going to let you imagine the questions and simply give you her answers.

"My background? Usual upper middle class. Education: a series of finishing schools. My present life is happy, uneventful, conventional. I have a husband, four children . . . I drive car pools . . . belong to a yacht club . . . a country club . . . breed German shepherds . . . garden . . . swim . . . sail. As a publicity girl once said to me: 'My God, you are *dull!*' And so I am. . . . But I don't like stress and disorder in my life or my work.

"I see writing as a series of problems to be solved not by flashes of insight but by steady, rational application. Incidentally, I have always written exactly what I pleased. . . .

"I have for many years made a comfortable income from my writing, though I don't need it . . . I've never believed that honest writing was de facto unsuccessful.

"I don't know why I started writing. In college I wrote a series of short stories, and a friend who was an established writer sent them to her agent. Alfred Knopf published the collection as *The Black Prince*. . . .

"I've never researched anything in my life. . . . I am a storyteller . . . a repository of odd bits of tales accumulated over the years from all kinds of places: newspapers, family stories, gossip. I remember and call on the information when I need it. An inefficient computer if you like.

"I have no set work hours, that's always seemed to me a foolish, arbitrary organization. . . . I work as much as I need to. Rewriting is the same: I do as much as I need to, but always at least one rewrite.

"People are coming back to fiction. They are feeling cramped by fact, and they are reaching out for something else. . . . Quality fiction, 'literary' if you must, is part of the whole search for meaning. . . . It is symbolic . . . it has something to say about life and hate and love and death. . . .

"I seldom write more than three or four hours a day. If I'm lucky I write while the children are at school . . . if not I write at night. . . . It's better to write every day once a book is started. It's easier then . . . you don't lose the thread.

"The short story depends on its delicacy, its perfection of line. Its value is in seeing the bones; it's like a high-fashion model. . . . But in a novel the last thing you want to see are the bones. If you did it would look unfinished.

"A novel's strength is in its overall effect, and when the reader has finished it he should be overwhelmed by that effect. Also, the bulk of the novel adds to its effectiveness.

"Too, there's an endless market for novels, whereas the market for short stories has decreased steadily. . . . Magazines that use fiction seem to be closing down one after another while the sale of novels, particularly in paperback, is booming.

"I never started out to be a writer. . . . I wanted to be a polo player when I was a girl. . . . It just broke my heart that I couldn't. . . . When I grew up in the late 1940s and in college in the fifties, there were darn few opportunities for girls. I liked law but it was almost completely closed. . . . Writing offered two things. . . . First there was no prejudice against women. In fact, being a woman has a slight advantage, especially in nonfiction. Not much, but a little. And second, writing was free and open. The regular kind of job, I wouldn't do—the kind with everything so organized. . . . So you see, I guess I became a writer by the process of elimination. . . .

"My family wasn't intellectual. . . . My father was a dentist . . . I was taught to read very early and we had an excellent library . . . but Thomas Hardy's works were too much for a young girl.

"When I was graduated from Newcomb, my father said I had to get a job or go to graduate school. . . . So I went to graduate school and that gave me a chance to lock myself up in my room and write stories.

"I took an apartment in the French quarter . . . it had black and purple walls and low fuzzy furniture . . . very chic I thought at the time. For a while I reversed day and night and found it marvelous. . . . I'd always wanted to do that, sleep in the day and work at night. But after you've been writing all night and you feel the need to relax and have a little company, at say five in the morning, well, it's pretty hard to find some of your friends in the mood to chat.

"When I won the Pulitzer for *The Keepers of the House*, I thought someone was playing a joke, because the first I heard of it was when a reporter for the *Times-Picayune* called and told me I'd won. So I called my publisher, Alfred Knopf, to verify. He, with his typical haughty air, said, 'Yes, it's true. You won it. It's no Nobel Prize, but I guess it will have to do for the time being.' I had felt absolutely great for five seconds, until his words began to sink in. Then I came down. . . . Alfred was right, really. The Nobel is the only prize that means anything, the only prize that carries any weight. . . .

"Usually, for a year and a half, the work on a new book isn't so intensive. . . . I sort of play with things, with ideas, with the plot. But I begin to pick up speed as I approach my self-imposed deadline.

"When you get bad reviews, the first ones hurt, sure. But after a while you accept them as a fact of life, and you don't pay any attention. What's really annoying is when the reviewer is right. There were some like that for *The Hard Blue Sky;* I could have kicked myself for not having made more changes before the book was published.

"It's gratifying that writing is the one thing you don't need formal training for. You've got to have training for law, and teaching, and welding, and for medicine, but not for writing . . . all you need is the innate ability to handle words. . . . As for creativity, we don't have the vaguest idea about creativity. . . . Either you have the desire to create, or you don't; and then you either create or you don't. We walk or we fall."

The following novels by Shirley Ann Grau are in paperback:
The Black Prince ● *The Condor Passes* ● *The Hard Blue Sky* ● *The House on Coliseum Street* ● *The Keepers of the House* ●

WRITE WHAT INTERESTS YOU
DONALD HAMILTON

Donald Hamilton tends to shun the title of author. "I am a professional writer," he says. "I write for a living."

His living has become a rather affluent one after some years in which he frankly admits his wife's income as a teacher was sometimes more than just a steadying influence on the economics of a four-child family.

Matt Helm, hero of seventeen intelligent, action-filled spy thrillers of Hamilton's authorship published under the Fawcett imprint, has done much to steady the fortunes of the Hamilton family, particularly since the series has been sold to the movies and several popular films in the series have appeared, with Dean Martin as Matt Helm. (More than 23,500,000 copies of this series are in print.)

However, it wasn't Matt Helm that brought Donald Hamilton out of writing obscurity. He made his first fame as a magazine fiction writer, and two of his early magazine serials were made into major motion pictures. The first was *Smoky Valley*, starring Glenn Ford, Edward G. Robinson, and Barbara Stanwyck; the second *Big Country*, with Gregory Peck, Burl Ives, Carroll Baker, and Charles Bickford.

Hamilton's decision to write was made after he graduated from the University of Chicago in 1938 with a degree in chemistry and had spent World War II as an officer specialist at the Naval Engineering Experiment Station in Annapolis, Maryland. Writing in his off hours he sold several short magazine pieces—an experience he relished more than anything he had ever done in the world of chemistry. "So," he said, "I'll be a writer."

"How did the idea ever enter your head?" he was asked. "How did it happen you wrote your first story?"

"I like to read other writer's stories, so I tried writing one and found it was even more fun to make up stories of my own."

See, it's as simple as that.

Actually, Hamilton had a number of lean years, but he kept his faith, writing what pleased him and having the pleasure of seeing his writings get ever-wider exposure and greater earnings as his markets expanded into motion pictures and foreign countries. And all this time he has developed his personal interests and written about them. He is a gun expert and an outdoorsman, and has written with some regularity in the outdoor magazine field. He loves sailing and boating, and has written about that. He is an expert photographer, and has written about that, and about hunting.

And all of these interests have played their part to interest and entertain readers in the many Matt Helm espionage books and in other books of his authorship. He has become, too, an expert on the old West, but confesses that many of his early western serials and novels were written before he achieved his "expert" rating.

He has now written more than two dozen mysteries, detective novels, espionage books, and westerns and several hundred short pieces for magazines.

Here's what he says about his manner of writing:

Q. How much time do you spend at the typewriter?

A. Three or four hours every morning when I have a book going, seven days a week. Even one day off means I lose the continuity and have to do a lot of rereading to catch up.

121

Q. What do you do toward preplanning a novel?

A. If you mean plotting, I don't. I just turn a couple of characters loose and follow them with the typewriter. All I know when I start is who they are and where they'll be operating; the rest pretty well takes care of itself. There's nothing deadlier than an outline; I've tried it. You wind up forcing a bunch of people to do what the outline says, rather than letting them do what comes naturally.

Q. But you have given some thought to those characters before you sit down to write.

A. Oh, sure. I've turned them over in my mind. I know who they are and how they will react in a given situation, and I know what they look like. They are completely fictional characters, but I may borrow a striking face from someone in real life, or an interesting mannerism.

Q. Do you know where they are going to operate—what part of the world?

A. Oh, sure, and I make a point of knowing everything I can about the locale, usually I have visited it. After spending a year in Sweden, for instance, it was only natural that I should lean on the inspiration button until a story evolved suitable for the fine Nordic scenery I had observed. That's what sparked *The Wrecking Crew.* More recently, after accompanying some anthropologists through a particularly grim and desolate corner of northern Mexico, I woke up one morning with a fine idea for a book that became *The Ambushers.*

Q. Does this mean your story ideas always spring from locale?

A. No, not always. A writer's plot may be something he dreamed up one sleepless night, but if he can lay his ideas against a background he knows and is interested in, chances are it will have freshness and interest for both writer and reader. Certainly the writer's handling of the geographical location is particularly important to the authentic feeling of a book. It's possible to get some notion of a place by reading about it or looking at pictures, but nothing takes the place of seeing it or living in it. For the novel I'm currently writing, I drove ten thousand miles up through Canada and came home with about four hundred color slides.

Q. You put a great deal of emphasis on authenticity.

A. Indeed I do. In a suspense novel particularly, where a

high degree of intelligence is expected of your hero—it had better be reflected in what the author says, too. Only careful research can give solidity to a suspense writer's work, particularly in the fields of tools and techniques. Nothing makes a grim, exciting, and presumably realistic scene of violence fall flat as fast as a reference to such nonexistent armament items as "automatic revolvers," (well, there was one once, but I've never seen one and I've seen a lot of guns) or revolvers with safety catches. (Automatics have safety catches, revolvers don't.) Similarly, if you put a Porsche engine in front or a Jaguar engine behind, the reader is liable to get the discouraging idea that you don't know what you are writing about, including any derring-do concerning your hero. Yes, every physical detail of the book must be rock-solid and factual, even if the plot, of some necessity, can't be.

Q. What, possibly, might be the most valuable advice you could give a beginning writer?

A. Whatever you choose to write, if it is to be good, you must respect it and you've got to believe in it—which means, essentially, that the stuff you write has to be the stuff you like to read.

To expand on that a bit, in fiction *how* you write is considerably more important than *what* you write. Most stories have been told before; telling them again isn't going to get you very far unless you can find a new and fresh way of doing it. But even the tiredest old plot can take on new life, written by someone eager and enthusiastic.

This being the case, you can't ever afford to pass up an idea that really excites you, because this is probably the idea you'll put your finest writing into. And your writing, in the last analysis, is all you have to sell.

If you want to be a professional writer, you simply can't afford to write for money or security or anything but the sheer pleasure of writing what you really like and writing it well.

So put your efforts into the stuff that fires your imagination. With a little luck you'll find, as I did, that the market requires exactly the stuff you turn out.

The following Donald Hamilton books are in paperback:
The Ambushers ● *The Betrayers* ● *Death of a Citizen* ● *The Devastators* ● *Interlopers* ● *The Intimidators* ● *The Intriguers* ● *The Menacers* ● *Murderers' Row* ● *The Poisoners* ● *The Ravagers* ● *The Removers* ● *The Retaliators* ● *The Shadowers* ● *The Silencers* ● *The Terminators* ● *The Wrecking Crew* ● *The Two-Shoot Gun* ● *Iron Men & Silver Stars* ●

A LETTER FROM "THE WELCOME STRANGER"

JANE AIKEN HODGE

"Jane Aiken Hodge is one of the better practitioners of the historical suspense-romance," says the San Francisco *Chronicle*, a mild understatement of her abilities. She has also written a factual book of great interest—*Only a Novel: The Double Life of Jane Austen.*

Mrs. Hodge was born in Boston, but lives in England now in a redesigned building that used to be a pub called, invitingly, "The Welcome Stranger." Here, in her own words, is how she became an author:

"Just for fun, I'll tell you how my first book got published. I'd been trying for a few years with British book publishers and no luck. Then my book was taken by Hale, and I only found out recently from someone in the company how it happened. There was a secretary there with whom I shared my name, Hodge. She read the submission, liked it, and brought it to the attention of the editors. Fancy that! I like to think Doubleday, in the States, may have taken it later for purer reasons."

Authors write splendid letters, as they should, and having one from Jane Aiken Hodge that answers all the questions I asked her, I want you to get it direct, unexcerpted, unexpurgated, the real thing:

Dear Mr. Daigh,

I have now got back from a splendid two-week holiday in Venice, dealt with the worst of the mail, and will try and give you a proper answer to your letter. But, first, I feel in honor bound to say that I disagree with your basic premise. It seems to me that too many books are written—and published—already, and I am therefore dubious about encouraging more people to write. But, on the other hand, as I look on writing as one of the major pleasures of life, I have to admit that the more people who can be introduced to it, the happier. So . . .

No, I absolutely do not use real people. Or, to be realistic, I do not do so consciously. This, in fact, is one of the reasons I like to write historical fiction; one is automatically at a safe remove from one's friends and acquaintances.

As to the plan of my books; this varies from one to another. For instance, *Savannah Purchase* turned out almost exactly as planned, while *The Winding Stair* turned upside down halfway through, but,

124

to my surprise, I found that I had already laid down the basis for the change, without noticing I was doing it. The "plan," by the way, tends to be a couple of pages, single spaced, extremely incoherent, and often abandoned halfway through when I start writing.

Research. I do a great deal. I reckon to start reading for the next book roughly when I am halfway through writing the last. The result is quite a thick file of extremely miscellaneous notes, which probably would make sense to no one but me. Before I actually start to write, I make myself a calendar for my period, remembering (I hope!) to take into account the length of time it took for news to get from place to place. For instance, in *Here Come a Candle* one had constantly to bear in mind that it took at least six weeks for news to get across the Atlantic. Hence the fact that the War of 1812 happened at all, and went on being fought after the peace was signed. The calendar, of course, will include both world and local events. A few items from the calendar for the book I've just started, *Mardale*, are: "Jan. Capture of Ciudad Rodrigo; March, Production of play, *Julius Caesar*, takes 5 hours. Easter Sunday, April 6th, Capture of Badajoz, n.b. two weeks or so for news from Spain." And so on. So, if you find my characters going to *Julius Caesar*, you'll know it was being played.

Favorite authors. Jane Austen. Charlotte Brontë. Anne Bridge. Georgette Heyer. These are ones whose influence I recognize, not by any means all of my favorites. For instance, I love Henry James but don't dare read him when I am writing because of the fatal influence of his style. In fact, when I am writing, I tend to do my background reading (diaries, letters, history) and subside into thrillers in the evening and at weekends.

I actually write for about two hours to three every morning, depending how it goes, and ruthlessly sitting down at 10, regardless of domestic calls. This produces 4 to 5 pages, somewhere between 1 and 2 thousand words. I reread the current chapter, revising, before I start. In the afternoon, I read, maybe another two or three hours. Weekends I never write.

Yes, I rewrite a lot, both as I go along, and after I have finished. And, in the end, one's publishers always have valuable suggestions which I have learned to respect. Pat Soliman at Coward–McCann did wonders for *Strangers in Company*, though I fought and convinced her on one point.

All my family write. My father's Conrad Aiken, my stepfather's a British poet and novelist. My sister Joan Aiken was established before I started, and my brother, John Aiken, has started since. Like, it's in the blood. I wrote a bad autobiographical novel when I was quite young. Thank God, no one would take it. Then, time out for marriage and a family. Started again when my second daughter started school. That was *Runaway Bride*, strongly influenced by Georgette Heyer. Then *Camilla* got taken for serial, but not, at the time, hard-backed (it's now *Marry in Haste*).

Oh, my life. Born Dec. 4, 1917, Boston, Mass. Moved to England at four. Educated here. B.A., Oxford (English Honors) 1938. Went on a voyage of exploration to the U.S. Fellowship at Radcliffe, A.M. 1939. Stayed on to work as research assistant to a psychologist, got caught by the war. A brief, unsuccessful first marriage took me to the University of Saskatchewan as a faculty wife, then to Washington, where I worked for the British Government. When we parted I went to New York and worked as a researcher for *Time*, which taught me a lot. Got homesick in 1947, came back to England, got a job with *Life* and married Alan Hodge, editor of *History Today*. Two daughters, one now working for Macmillan, the other at Oxford. I've read for publishers and Warner Bros. and done some reviewing. Last year I bought us this house, which used to be a pub called The Welcome Stranger, and we all commute to and fro between here and Wimbledon. I now have a study of my own, instead of working in the family sitting room. It makes a remarkable difference.

I do hope this gives you something of what you asked for.

Yours sincerely,
Jane Aiken Hodge.

The following are in paperback:
Greek Wedding ● *Marry in Haste* ● *Only a Novel: The Double Life of Jane Austen* ● *Runaway Bridge* ● *Savannah Purchase* ● *Shadow of a Lady* ● *Strangers in Company* ● *Watch the Wall, My Darling* ● *The Winding Stair* ●

THE TOP HAND WITH WESTERNS
LOUIS L'AMOUR

The most popular, and largest selling, living author of the western novel is this self-educated adventurer whose name has a memorable distinction of sorts, because it would seem more at home on a French perfume than a novel about cowboys, Indians, and rustlers. Some of his family spell it "LaMoore." Louis was born in North Dakota and spent the first fifteen years of his life there, before becoming a school dropout.

"I spent those years," he says, "reading everything in sight and walking the hills with a rifle. Most of my study periods were devoted to tracing out routes on maps of the world that I someday intended to follow.

"And I didn't have as long to wait for those trips as I thought. Halfway through the tenth grade my father's economic situation became such that no objections were raised to my leaving school, and I started traveling."

In the fifteen years that followed, he knocked around in the West Indies, Europe, Japan, China, the East Indies, South Pacific Islands, the Straits Settlements, Burma, Arabia, Egypt, and Latin America. And he adds almost casually, "I walked and rode a bicycle across India."

And how was all this financed?

"I did almost anything for pay, including work as a miner, lumberjack, sawmill hand, circus roughneck, tourist guide, construction worker, and boxer."

He also admits to having ridden freight trains, stowing away on ships, prospecting for gold, hunting for buried treasure, and exploring a lot of country "just for the hell of it."

"I missed a lot of meals," he admits, "slept on lumber piles, in empty boxcars, had a lot of waterfront brawls, but never started any."

He was the right age for World War II, going in as a private and coming out a first lieutenant in the Tank Destroyers. He was in England, France, Belgium, Holland, and Germany.

And after all that knocking about, his advice to would-be writers includes: "Don't go out seeking experiences so you can write about them. Experience is valuable, but anyone who deliberately seeks it out destroys its value. One must draw on the stuff of living, but one must live with *awareness*. This is the key word."

Louis is an avid searcher for genuine old-timers of the West, and when he finds one he will interview him on a tape recorder for hours, recording the oldster's recollections and anecdotes. He collects diaries and old books about the early West and puts in many hours researching facts on the old West in reference libraries.

He has written sixty-five novels to date and is translated into seventeen languages, with more than 50 million copies sold. His movies include *Hondo, East of Sumatra, Heller in Pink Tights, Stranger on Horseback, The Tall Stranger, Utah Blaine, Shalako, Catlow, Man Called Noon*, and many others.

Louis has been until quite recently exclusively a writer of original paperbacks, but is doing some hardcover books for *Saturday Review Press*. In a recent letter he casually mentions the following about his plans: "I have launched a project that has actually been going on unannounced for some time, a project to tell the story of the American frontier in about forty novels. I shall tell it all through the eyes of three families and successive generations—bringing them over from England, Ireland, and France—with assorted intermarriages, some of them with exotic types."

The Western novel is, of course, thoroughly American and has been called the only category of literature that had its origin in the United States. Certainly Louis L'Amour is a master of this kind of novel. Everything about his novels reflects honesty of characters, honesty of locale, honesty in every detail, and stories that relate honest emotion. "Authenticity" is the usual word, but with Louis L'Amour "honesty" seems the right one.

If your ambition is to write a western novel, I do hope the colorful background and outstanding achievements of this best-of-them-all will not intimidate you. There's room for many more writers of westerns.

The following is directly from the Man himself. He wants to help.

"If you are going to be a writer the first essential is just to write; write whenever, wherever, however, but write.

"Do not wait for an idea. Start writing something and the ideas will come. You have to turn the faucet on before the water starts to flow.

"Writing is my profession, and to me the highest compliment a writer can receive is to be told he is a 'pro.' Shakespeare was. He wrote for a theater in which he had invested, and he wrote to please an audience. One reason his stuff has lasted, aside from the grace and beauty of his poetry and the way in which he used words, is simply that he wrote for an audience, and he used timeless themes. Shakespeare dealt with love, hate, revenge, jealousy, ambition . . . and they are always with us.

"I do not plot my stories. I found this useful training in the beginning, but now I take a character or group of characters and put him or them into a situation and let them react. I have had a wide experience with living, fighting, working. I know the type of men of whom I write, so I believe I can interpret them correctly. No matter what style of story one wishes to do, the writer should stay with people he knows.

"As to characters: I rarely use real people as such. The people in my books are typical of real people. They are like people I have known, but they are my own invention. The problems are real-life problems and I place the people in situations that exist.

"I think about a story, think about the people (to me they are people, not characters) and I get the locale fixed firmly in my mind if it was not so before.

"I do no rewriting. Formerly I did some rewriting, but for me it is best to let the story flow. I grew up on storytelling and it is a natural thing for me to do, but the technique must be learned. It does not happen.

"I work on an IBM typewriter. I eat breakfast and begin work at once. I work never less than five hours a day at the typewriter, that is, occasionally as much as fourteen. I like my work. I have to guard against getting too involved in research and not writing as much as I should.

"I have no hobbies. Hobbies are for idle time and I have none. All my activities: hiking, shooting, tracking, learning about plants and animals are geared to my work.

"Research to be good must come from original sources, and there are many: historical societies, old newspaper files, genealogical societies, diaries, journals, letters, and, most valuable of all, on-the-spot observation.

"Two of the best authors for young writers to read are O. Henry and Robert Louis Stevenson. Both are supreme technicians. Stevenson and Anthony Trollope wrote with intelligence about writing. All were craftsmen in the best sense and knew what they were doing.

"As to discipline: my wife says I am the most disciplined person she knows, and she sees me more than anyone else and has been with me through many books.

"Writing and all that attends it is my greatest pleasure; my schedule might seem very rough to some, but to me it is the essence of living."

Following are the author's books in paperback:
Crossfire Trail ● *Heller with a Gun* ● *Hondo* ● *Kilkenny* ● *Last Stand at Papago Wells* ● *Showdown at Yellow Butte* ● *The Tall Stranger* ● *To Tame a Land* ● *Utah Blaine* ●

TOPS IN HISTORICAL ROMANCE
NORAH LOFTS

Norah Lofts is an English author whose historical romances have gained instant popularity in the United States. Hers is the true storyteller's art, an almost hypnotic skill that carries her reader into eighteenth century England as though it were part of the reader's living experience. She is particularly skilled in interpreting the period by unobtrusive references to customs of the day, objects of the household, and the costumes that were worn. Real kings and queens and others famed in history populate her books, along with fictional characters who seem as real as those buried in Westminster Abbey. Like William Faulkner, she has invented locales where many of her characters reside, in book after book, Baildon and Layer Wood.

Here is an author who wrote her first book, evenings and holidays, while holding a full-time job as a teacher in an English girls' school; thus she was primarily occupied with teaching and grading papers of more than sixty students.

It took Norah Lofts five years to sell her first book. But once she sold it, she quit teaching to write another, and another, until she has now written more than two dozen.

When faced with constructing a new book, she confesses to a sort of "daydreaming" period, when people and ideas float around in her consciousness, becoming more and more firm and real as she indulges her reverie. She is particularly partial to such imaginings while in her bath or while being driven about in a car. Once the book has taken some form in her mind, she writes at a desk in the corner of a room with a blank wall before her. She works a long day, usually seven days each week.

The following are excerpts from a letter she sent at my invitation:

The letter was headed, "I *Do* Hope This Helps Someone Who Wants to Write."

So far as I know nothing in my family background made me a writer. Though there perhaps I wronged my paternal grandfather; I spent a good deal of time with him when I was young, and being the child of his youngest son, I was young when he was getting old and valued peace and quiet. So he gave me a box of colored chalks and a lot of paper. This is odd; I always drew houses—and houses have run through my real life, through my dreams, through my books—a recurrent theme. I drew people, too, in and around the houses, and my poor grandfather did not attain the hoped-for peace; I began to tell him what the tiny match-stalk woman at the bedroom window said to the tiny match-stalk boy outside the front door and what he said to her. Not surprisingly, when I went home after that holiday, I carried with me a letter for my father. It was brief. It said, "This child should learn to read and write." My father was a very busy man—a farmer—but he was an obedient son and proceeded to teach me these arts. I was four at the time, and I think I may truthfully say that in the intervening sixty-five years I have never been a nuisance to anybody in the way of chatter or demands for attention. I take a book wherever I go. The train may be late, the queue at the doctor's or the dentist's long, but I don't even notice. There is always a conscientious character waiting to alert me. Having discovered writing at this young age I began to write. I wrote stories and sewed the pages into cardboard covers and presented them at Christmas and on other occasions. Not one of these has survived, so I gather that they weren't taken very seriously. Around 1930, when in my twenties, I began to cherish immoderate ambitions. I wrote my first book, *I Met a Gypsy*. (At the time I was doing a full-time teaching job and wrote in the evenings and through the holidays.) Then came my efforts at marketing the manuscript; I was so hog-ignorant I did not know that publishers specialized as to the type of books they published.

The story came home so often that it was known as "Norah's Homing Pigeon" and my family, who regarded this obsession with writing and selling a book as an amiable eccentricity, would sometimes hide it in case my classes (sixty strong in those days!) had worn me down a bit. It would be produced at the appropriate moment when I was somewhat exuberant and could take the sorrow of another rejection. This went on for five years.

Sometimes I took the manuscript up to London and from various publishing houses I, with it, was summarily kicked out. One man, who shall be nameless, after asking what I did for a living, told me that my function in life was to teach children to read, not to provide reading matter for adults. (All right, I can laugh now; he is no longer in business and the book is still alive, but, as you see, the scar still aches.)

Anyway, in 1935 I did find a publisher and got an advance of £20. All the bells of heaven rang. The book was well-reviewed—believe it or not and forgive me—in time of famine one must remember time of feast. I think it was *The Observer* which said, "I can give it no higher praise than to say that it calls Thornton Wilder to mind." And

131

dear Raymond Postgate—dead now, and may the earth lay lightly on him—was talent-scouting for Knopf's in New York. They took it; and one day in 1936 sent me a cheque that amounted to my teacher's salary for a year. The book had also been well-reviewed on your side.

Meanwhile, I had married—to a man sensitive enough to give me a typewriter as a wedding present. Previously, I had hired one. So then I thought—I'll take a sabbatical year, not write in a rather hole-and-corner way just for a year; if it doesn't work out I'll go back and teach.

I never went back. And, honestly, maybe that was a pity. In this town in which, with the briefest intermissions, I have spent my life, there are dozens of women, middle-aged now, who can write a good letter and address it correctly, who can read books and enjoy them, coaxed as they were to *Precious Bane, Jane Eyre,* and *The Cloister and the Hearth* by me, their teacher. But perhaps if I had stayed on I should have been sacked—teachers are not now allowed to teach children to spell or punctuate or to sit and be read to.

I do not believe I am influenced by other writers. I read a great deal. There are writers whom I admire very much; there are times when I think, "God, I wish I could write like this. . . ." But it can't be done. N. Lofts must write as N. Lofts. (Oddly enough, by the same post that brought your letter came one from an American woman who said she believed that she would know one of my books if my name were not on it. That kind of thing in writers of greater reputation is known as "style." With me it is, "Oh. N. Lofts has been at it again.")

My working day is long. I sit down at 9 A.M. and rise at 1. I resume at 4:30, and go until 7:30. I do this every day of the week, practically every day of the year. The exceptions are when I have visitors, especially my family which includes a child of three-plus, who has an absolute passion for this machine. When she is under my roof, it has to be put away; with grown-up visitors I am rather apt to say, "Oh, go take a walk; look at the ruins!" It would be idle to pretend that all the typing which a seven-hour day produces is immortal prose; but it keeps my fingers in going order and usually, except for the pages which go into the wastepaper basket, something is worth keeping—some glimmer of an idea, some unsuspected glimpse of character. Yes, I do rewrite a lot; I begin the day by reading what was done yesterday and then often rewrite, cutting out exuberances and idle fancies, pruning adjectives. (One thing Somerset Maugham once said has had an effect on me: "Write as though you were sending a telegram." And that is sound advice for everybody; I mean, if you write, "Damn you to hell, you bastard," as a piece in a conversation, it really is a waste to add, "He said angrily.")

The kind of research I do, and the amount, depends entirely upon the type of book I am doing. Some, like *Bless This House* and the *House Trilogy* needed no more than standard history books. Trevelyan is a standby; Churchill's *History of the English-Speaking Peoples*—that kind of thing; and of course I read things like *Food in England* and *History of the English Carriage*. I have just, admittedly a bit late in life, invested £7.35 in a book called *Time of Feast, Time of Famine,* which gives details of climate over the last 1,000 years. (Maybe that was a mistake, because in future I shall not be able to command the weather and write, "It was a bad harvest that year." This will distress me because I do like to be in control.) But there are books which demand something more. I am fortunate in that I live within twenty-six miles of the University Library at Cambridge; I have spent many useful, if not happy, hours there. Not happy because one is not allowed to smoke—and I smoke whenever I read or write—also all the other library inmates appear to have been dead for quite a long time. For three books, *The Lost Queen*, *A Rose for Virtue* and *Crown of Aloes*, I have been obliged to ask for help from outside for two reasons; apart from *just* enough French to ask directions from A to B, I am monolingual, and for these books it was necessary to consult papers and books not available in English; also I now can't do much of what is called "legwork." Of research I would say to any aspiring writer, do it and forget it! Nothing bores the general reader—I know, being one—more than the obtrusion, the look-how-well-I-did-my-homework! Sweat is a healthy thing, but it should be wiped away.

This is, I am sure, the most revealing thing I have ever written about myself. I do hope I do not sound a bit arrogant. That I would deplore. The point is there was this one thing that I could do; in so many areas I am so inept: I can't drive a car, read a railway timetable, tell a share from a stock, mend a fuse, or work out a date. I am "innumerate," just as some people are illiterate, but people who cannot add, subtract, and divide are despised, while those who cannot read are pitied and given special teachers. It is an odd world and will get odder. But this I do believe . . . even if we are headed back to the cave (and there is every indication that we are—oil is about to run out) someday, somebody, necessarily old in order to have such memory will say, "Sit down and I will tell you a story. . . ." I know what is called the oldest profession, but I think mine is older!

For purposes of my lifework I was born at the right place—a farm—and at the right time, 1904. Change comes slowly in country places, and it takes me very little effort to imagine even eighteenth-century life. I had eight blissfully happy years, dogs, ponies, wild flowers; then my father d¹ed, leaving my mother with four of us. I was the oldest. We had a wonderful mother who did not sit down and weep and sponge on her relatives. She came into this town and took boarders, and she gave us all (these were the days when nothing was free) as much education as we could take. I couldn't get to University because in those days a certain standard in mathematics was required before one could matriculate, and as I mentioned I am blind to numbers, but I was welcomed at a Training College for teachers. I taught. I was married. I have one son who shares my love of books but has not so far shown any desire to write one. I was widowed. I married a second time.

I now live in a house which bitchy people—not all female by any means—call a mansion. Actually, it is nothing of the sort. It's old and it's beautiful and it was unwanted. Nobody would buy it—it was going to be made into a tax office! Everybody thought, and some said, that I was mad; and I must admit that when the rain came in, I thought I was mad too. But it contains four rather nice flats, houses me, my husband, my sister, a Hungarian refugee who cooks after a fashion, and three dogs. It is the third old house I have rescued in my time; and if I do not leave the world a better place than I found it, I shall leave it cleaner—I have installed six bathrooms from scratch. This house must have been "modernized" about one hundred years ago; there is what must have been the first W C in Bury. There is a most endearing little china plaque on the door of the downstairs cloakroom which reads, "Pull and let go." I suppose the installers feared that somebody might pull and then stand there until he/she dropped dead of old age. I do rather cherish that.

Bury St. Edmund's is, of course, my place; but in my books I call it Baildon. I can't say why, the name just popped into my head and I didn't know until quite recently that there is a town of that name in Yorkshire. Calling my town by another name is a defensive measure; no matter how much you know there is always somebody who knows a little bit more, and if I wrote about Bury St. Edmund's and mentioned somebody's tripping over the cobbles in December 1781, up would pop this know-it-all and say that he knew for a fact that all the cobblestones were removed from Bury streets in July 1781. And I do like elbow room. So I made my own geography, and it is curious how people respond. There is this Layer Wood, about which so many of my books center. (It does exist, I gathered oxlips and bluebells in it.) But people write from places like Texas and say

134

that they can see and smell Layer Wood; or that the moment they see the name they know that they are going to like the book.

People write otherwise, too. I will give you an example—a moral for the young. In one of the House books I made an ardent Methodist say, "As the hymn says, we must take it to the Lord in prayer." Nothing happened for quite a long time and then I had (from Malaya of all places) a rebuke, one of these, Dear Miss Lofts, I enjoyed your book, but . . . But! Oh dear, my man had quoted the hymn before it was written, and somebody in Malaya had spotted it.

Books by Norah Lofts, published in paperback, include:
Crown of Aloes ● *The Concubine* ● *Eleanor the Queen* ● *The House at Old Vine* ● *The House at Sunset* ● *How Far to Bethlehem* ● *Jassy* ● *The King's Pleasure* ● *Little Wax Doll* ● *The Lost Queen* ● *Lovers All Untrue* ● *The Lute Player* ● *Nethergate* ● *Out of the Dark* ● *A Rose for Virtue* ● *Scent of Cloves* ● *The Town House* ● *Winter Harvest* ●

AN AUTHOR WITH A FAN CLUB
JOHN D. MacDONALD

Travis McGee, fictional hero of seventeen colorful crime-suspense novels, is possibly the best-known fiction hero of any suspense series written by a living author. John D. MacDonald is his creator. Travis lounges about on a houseboat, The Busted Flush, somewhere in Florida while waiting for opportunities to help damsels in distress—attractive damsels, that is. John D., the author, does very little lounging, but he has an excellent place to do it if he ever so chooses, also in Florida. The potential lounging place is a huge second-floor porch, extending almost entirely around his large self-designed vaguely octagonal, vaguely Polynesian-style house on stilts, exclusively situated on a tongue of land overlooking what may be the only stretch of genuine white water in all of Florida. The porch is superbly equipped for lounging with double-size rope hammocks.

All of which you can aspire to if you write, as he has, more than fifty successful novels, at a pace of more than two a year; a pace that left him little time for lounging.

Perhaps it is a trait John picked up while acquiring an M.B.A. at the Harvard Business School, but he is an author who chose to bypass hardcover publication for his novels and write original paperbacks; and thus not share his reprint royalties with a hardcover publisher. Now, in confirmation of his judgment, E. P. Dutton is bringing out both the earlier and the new Travis McGee books in hardcovers to excellent reviews and a very large and responsive audience. All royalty checks from hard- and soft-cover are made out to "John D. MacDonald."

So loyal and appreciative are his readers they have formed what must be the only one-author fan club, complete with magazine, in the world. The club and magazine operate from the West Coast. John supplies gratitude for such appreciation and a now-and-then letter for the magazine, but that is the extent of his connection. It is a sincere, genuine response by his fans and is in no way connected with press agentry.

Read what this master of suspense has to say about his craft:

Writing is my trade and my joy and my despair, depending on how well or how poorly it seems to be going at any given moment.

I cannot imagine ever doing anything else.

Yet I had no idea of actually being a writer until I was twenty-nine. I read everything I could reach from the day I learned to read. I thought that to be an author would be the best thing anyone could ever do—to put down the words for others to read. But I did not think it could ever be me. Not ever.

I wrote things, but it was as if I were imitating a writer, and thus it was a secret vice. It was not until almost half a life had passed that I realized all writers who share this same compulsion, this same dream, have the hidden, guilty suspicion that they are merely giving an imitation of what they hope to become.

Because I had an inner listlessness about what I would do with my life, I responded easily to what my father hoped I would do. I went to the Wharton School of Finance and dropped out after almost two years, worked at small weird jobs in New York City, finally reentered college at Syracuse, got a B.S. in Business Administration, married Dorothy, went to Harvard Business School, received an M.B.A. in Business Administration, sired a son, went to work, got fired with alarming frequency, went into the army for five-and-a-half years and came back from overseas with three months' accumulated leave and a terminal promotion to Lieutenant Colonel.

The army had cured me, or partially cured me, of that malady which had gotten me fired so regularly—a virulent case of Boca Grande (Big Mouth)—and in the normal course of events I would have fitted myself back into the business world, carefully and diligently, yet without joy.

But great luck rescued me from my own blindness about myself. Luck and Dorothy. During the last of my two-and-a-half years overseas, I was with OSS in the China-Burma-India Theater. At one point, due to the secret nature of ongoing operations, we were advised that outgoing mail was being subjected to one hundred percent censorship rather than the usual spot check, and that it would be best if no mention were made in letters of climate, foliage, health, food, friends, and so forth.

It made letters grotesquely difficult to write, and as a relief valve, I wrote a short story in longhand about some people in New Delhi, a place where I was no longer stationed. I wrote it to amuse Dorothy and to give her more of the special flavor of India than I could manage in straight exposition.

It got through, and without writing me what she was doing, she typed it in suitable form and submitted it first to *Esquire*, where it elicited a personalized and encouraging rejection rather than a form. Next she sent it to *Story* Magazine, where Whit Burnett purchased it for twenty-five dollars and, months later, published it under the title "Interlude in India."

When I was set free at Fort Dix, we had a rent-controlled apartment in Utica, New York, three months' leave, and tentative appointments my father had made for me with several corporations.

It seemed a good time to try to be a writer. Dorothy encouraged me. No one else did. During the winter of 1945-46, in four months—October, November, December, and January—I worked twelve and fourteen hours a day, seven days a week, and completed 800,000 words of typed manuscript. In February I sold a second story after months of keeping at least thirty stories in the mail to the magazines at all times. I had papered most of my small workroom with form rejection slips, and I painted them out when at last they began to really depress me. I lost twenty pounds. Relatives and friends discussed John's "severe readjustment problems." In short-story format I wrote the equivalent of ten full-length books in four months. Motivation was so overwhelming, I compressed years of learning into a brief time. By the end of 1946 we could just barely live on the income from writing. In 1947 extreme financial pressures were eased.

I am still learning. And I still feel as if I were almost a writer. One cannot apply linear logic to erase a deep suspicion that one is an impostor.

It is the memory of the amount of work it took to learn my trade that oftentimes makes me less than tolerant with the stranger who says earnestly, as though we share something special, "You know, I've always wanted to write!"

When my mood is especially astringent, I answer, "Really! I've always wanted to be a brain surgeon." The lay person can remove a splinter from a finger and can write a nice letter to Aunt Alice.

The most common question is, "Where do you get your ideas?"

I do not know where ideas come from. I have the feeling that somewhere in the back of my head there is an ancient cauldron where all the input of the years of my life boils and bubbles, with the random bits of things seen, felt, read, heard, discussed, all tumble together in ferment, appearing and disappearing atop the dark brew.

The thing which differentiates the human brain from the computer is the talent, or knack, or quirk, which the brain has for established logical and also illogical relationships. Emotion, humor, fear, hate—all these seem to come from unlikely juxtapositions of random bits in the storage banks, or in the cauldron, or whatever you want to call it.

The contents of the cauldron are not readily accessible to me until two or more random bits clot together in some associational relationship and float to the surface. Then I can take these items out, a coagulation, and turn the lump this way and that until I see a pattern that may or may not become a story.

The other day I retrieved some information bits in strange shape and form. A man once told me how he had fabricated his qualifications and made a quantum leap—forward or backward —from cab driver to assistant pursor on a cruise ship, and how, by mumbling and by writing in such a way no one could read it, he had successfully covered his areas of total ignorance until he learned the job on the job. I once saw a ship's officer get out of a cable car in American Samoa, pallid and wet and visibly shaken, perhaps because by chance he was the only passenger aboard on that six minute, gut-wrenching trip. I had read somewhere about a myna bird who lived next door to a fire house, and who learned such a persuasive imitation of the alarm bells and buzzers, he could fake out the firemen. In the thick offshore smoke of the burning Everglades a few years ago, birds landed on our small boat, some of them too near death from exhaustion to be saved.

I examined this curious clotting of four unrelated things. I know there has to be some connective—something in my mind which makes some congruent relationship—faking, loneliness, fright, imitation, communication.

When I perceive the relationships, then this might become a story or an incident within a story. My fallow periods occur when all the lumps I retrieve either have too apparent and simpleminded a relationship, or ones so complex they are beyond conscious perception.

138

After I have the idea for a novel, the idea will determine the approach and the length. A story is something happening to somebody. If the change is physical, environmental, then it is a casual and trivial story. I must qualify this by saying that there are some monstrous exceptions, such as Kafka's *Metamorphosis*. If the change is deep and subjective and lasting, then the story can have as much power as is within the capacities of the novelist.

Once I have the story, along with that prickling feeling of anticipation which clues me as to how well I might be able to do it, I establish a clear sense of the ending, and then I try, through trial and error, to find the most useful beginning. The right point in time to start a story is tricky. Begin too far back from the dramatic peaks and the story becomes slow and labored. Begin too close to the tensions and the pace becomes frantic. There are no rules except the subjective sense of "feel." I revise by throwing away. I might, for example, throw away thirty thousand words of a novel in first draft because it begins to feel progressively worse and beyond repair. Or I might discard the final twenty thousand of the first fifty thousand words by rereading it enough times to be able to detect the approximate arena where it began to feel wrong.

I do not plan the middle portions of a book. Once I have found a solid beginning-place, and know where it will end, I then have multiple choices of how to find my way through the thickets and jungles of the middle portion. When such portions get too far off the track because a side trail becomes too enticing, I can take out that portion and set it aside as something to read over the next time I am in the process of selecting a story to write. For me, too much preplanning destroys freshness and spoils my own fun. I do not know what each day of work will bring. I know the compass direction, but not the specific destination of each day.

Nobody ever invented a character, whether protagonist or walk-on, out of whole cloth. I have never consciously patterned any character after any specific person I know. I assemble the odds and ends of input into the people in the books, and then they become alive to me to the point where, when I attempt to manipulate them into word or deed which does not fit, the words go flat and the deeds are fumbled.

When a character is not consistent with his own patterns and habits and style, then the reader becomes all too aware of the fact that he is reading a book. The writer's hand has become visible, tugging at the strings, contriving scene and situation.

I strive for realism while knowing at all times that I can achieve the illusion of realism, not realism itself. Selectivity in description imitates reality. It shows the reader what you want him to see. If I describe a boat by saying, "Below decks she smelled of stale grease, stale urine, and old laundry," I need not mention the condition of the brightwork or running gear topside.

Yet in these shorthand techniques of realistic writing, I must be careful not to make the writing too vivid, or once again I intrude. The flamboyant overblown simile or analogy is like tapping the reader on the shoulder and saying, "Look how beautiful I'm writing, fella!"

I achieve a further illusion of realism by trying never to write about places I have never been and by researching the nuts-and-bolts details of various skills, occupations, and professions where appropriate.

A further aspect of realism is the result of the writer's attitude toward his work. I know that I am involved in entertainment, but I also know that the more entertaining a book is the more readers it will reach, and if the entertainment is built upon some solid foundations of awareness of the world, then there will be a resonance about the work which can in certain ways alter the internal climate and the outward perceptions of the reader.

The fact of a writer taking himself seriously does not make of him a "serious" writer. Yet if he has any slight feeling that in his choice of materials or choice of approach he is patronizing and deluding the readership, then the flavor of truth and purpose and reality will drain out of his work. As literary history has shown us often and forcefully, critical acclaim has far less to do with lasting acceptance than does the internal disciplines of the work itself.

As regards the area in which I have often chosen to write, I would like to quote Nicholas Freeling: "We are all murderers, we are all spies, we are all criminals, and to choose a crime as the mainspring of a book's action is only to find one of the simplest methods of focusing eyes on our life and our world."

I have explained where I think the ideas come from and what I do with them once I have them reasonably well in hand. But I have not said anything about my appraisal of my own body of work. It is to me a long, tough, satisfying process of becoming. I have more control of my materials this year than I had last year. When the control improves, one can attempt the more delicate and sinuous confrontations without the dreadful risk of descending into inadvertent parody or situational grotesqueries. I have not done a book or a story that I could not now do more effectively.

There are internal rhythms in prose which tap the subjective emotional quotient of the reader, and create awareness of the identities of the human condition on many levels. These rhythms arise from the careful and selective simplicities, not from arcane juxtapositions. The words and the phrases are the architecture and the music. The more simple, the more elegant and effective. The more complex and intricate, the more self-conscious and ineffective. I keep the learning process going by writing poetry.

I will do as many more stories as time, energy, and self-knowledge will permit. It has meant sixty hours a week at this machine for more years than I care to confess. But there is not a day that I cannot get a quick, electric feeling of joyous anticipation when I roll the white empty page into the machine. A day, a week, a month, or a half year of work may leave me without a page I can keep. But sooner or later there will be a day when the satisfaction at the end of the day matches the anticipation at the beginning.

. And that's what keeps my machine running.

Almost all of John D. MacDonald's books are in paperback:

Travis McGee Series: *Bright Orange for the Shroud* ● *Darker Than Amber* ● *A Deadly Shade of Gold* ● *The Deep Blue Good-by* ● *The Dreadful Lemon Sky* ● *Dress Her in Indigo* ● *The Girl in the Plain Brown Wrapper* ● *The Long Lavender Look* ● *Nightmare in Pink* ● *One Fearful Yellow Eye* ● *Pale Gray for Guilt* ● *A Purple Place for Dying* ● *The Quick Red Fox* ● *The Scarlet Ruse* ● *Tan and Sandy Silence* ● *The Turquoise Lament* ●

Other MacDonald titles: *All These Condemned* ● *April Evil* ● *Area of Suspicion* ● *Ballroom of the Skies* ● *The Brass Cupcake* ● *A Bullet for Cinderella* ● *Cancel All Our Vows* ● *Clemmie* ● *Contrary Pleasure* ● *The Crossroads* ● *Cry Hard, Cry Fast* ● *The Damned* ● *Dead Low Tide* ● *Deadly Welcome* ● *Death Trap* ● *The Deceivers* ● *The Drowner* ● *The Empty Trap* ● *The End of the Night* ● *The Executioners* ● *Flash of Green* ● *The Girl, the Gold Watch & Everything* ● *The House Guests* ● *Judge Me Not* ● *A Key to the Suite* ● *The Last One Left* ● *A Man of Affairs* ● *Murder for the Bride* ● *Murder in the Wind* ● *The Neon Jungle* ● *One Monday We Killed Them All* ● *Please Write for Details* ● *The Price of Murder* ● *S E V E N* ● *Slam the Big Door* ● *Soft Touch* ● *You Live Once* ● *Where Is Janice Gantry?* ●

ONCE A LIBRARIAN
HELEN MacINNES

Helen MacInnes has been aptly called "one of the most successful novelists alive" and has reached this pinnacle from having written a total of only seventeen novels in about thirty-five years, every one of which has made the best-seller list. She is particularly cheered that each new book in hardcover outsells its predecessor; and having a fine eye for "reasons why," she has been generous in her praise of the effect the paperback editions have had on her ever-mounting hardcover sales. "I do want to thank you," she wrote in that respect. "As you find more and more readers for me in the cheaper editions, it is obvious many of these new readers are buying the new hardcover editions as they are published." Currently more than seventeen million copies of her books have been printed in Fawcett paperbacks.

Her success as an author is further distinguished because she has won her popularity without catering to what *Current Biography* identified as "the widespread taste for obscenity, sadism, and science fiction gadgetry." She does indeed write "clean" books, but they do not suffer from any lack of realism. Each of her novels can be categorized as romantic, action-filled stories of espionage, and many of them expose postwar communist efforts to undermine democracy in the United States and the harsh, inhuman dictates of communism in the occupied countries. Her realistic interpretation of the communist threat has a great deal to do with the continued success of her novels.

Miss MacInnes characterizes herself as being inclined to Jeffersonian democracy and opposed to all forms of totalitarianism—Nazi, Fascist, and Communist. She was born in Scotland and spent all of her formative years in Scotland, England, and the Continent and was a firsthand, close observer of the rise of the fascist and communist rule.

Her books from the first have displayed a simple approach and theme that is sterling in its attractiveness and usefulness to any ambitious author. The fact that her books do contain an active preachment of a political nature and are still fabulously successful is a tribute to her writing skill; the ideology never interferes with the warm and human story.

Her first novel, *Above Suspicion*, was published in 1941, after having been written in pencil in longhand. Gilbert Highet, her husband, recently retired as Professor of Latin and Greek at Columbia University, but then a teacher at Oxford, read it and said, "Not bad," she recalls. "So I went ahead and typed it, then I sent it off to Gilbert's agent (her husband had published) and in four days they accepted it. I think he was rather surprised. Then later on, of course, I got my galleys, and Gilbert told me I had to correct them myself. I was astonished. 'You mean I have to do this? But I am the author!' "

The plot summary of this first novel is a model of concise, guaranteed human interest story material and is stated thus:

An attractive English couple, being above suspicion, are sent to Germany seemingly on a vacation trip in the summer of 1939, just before the outbreak of World War II, to find a missing British anti-Nazi agent.

Anyone attempting to teach the contemporary suspense novel might well use that short paragraph above as the idealized example and model of how a full novel can be summarized in digest fashion and, at the same time, reflect a storytelling potential for thrilling events to happen against a background of danger and urgency.

I urge you to go back and read that short paragraph again. If your desire is to write suspense novels and you can state your story idea with as few words and as many promises as is contrived in the above, you are on your way.

It should be remarked that her preoccupation with the Nazi regime was a natural and ever-building personal interest, one that took on a hobby identity, somewhat like (but a more deadly subject than) stamp collecting. In the 1930s she had begun to keep a diary in which she recorded newspaper accounts of Hitler's rise to power and the strengthening Nazi party. She analyzed these frightening events and made her own predictions. There had been one halfhearted effort at writing a novel when she and her husband were at Oxford, but she reports she did not have the confidence to work seriously at writing it. It wasn't until she was thirty-two years old and living in New York with her husband, that he read over her diary notes and suggested that the time had come for her to write the novel she had frequently talked about writing sometime.

What happened to that first novel is as exciting as a novel itself. Critics had great praise for it. The New York *Herald Tribune* reviewer wrote glowingly: "Although a first novel, it tells an exciting story with the technical smoothness of an accomplished writer; it creates a mood of suspense which carries through to the end, and it possesses what is rare in a book of this sort, a subtle note of humor which contributes to the job." *Above Suspicion* was a selection of the

Book-of-the-Month Club, a flattering achievement for a first novel, and it was made into a hit motion picture starring Fred MacMurray and Joan Crawford.

And just to show the first novel wasn't a fluke, her next book, *Assignment in Brittany* was a best-seller and was made into a motion picture also, this one starring Susan Peters and Jean-Pierre Aumont.

Any provocative and preferably simple set of circumstances is likely to set this author off on a new espionage novel. *The Double Image*, another in the continuous succession of successful books, was prompted by a newspaper account that grabbed her interest—a report that the supposed grave of a Nazi war criminal had been found empty. In contemplating possible answers to this puzzle she seized on the theory of "double agent," the type of espionage operator who sells his services to both sides as did the Nazi-Soviet real-life agent, Richard Sorge. She insists the technical knowledge about espionage reflected in her novels comes from newspaper accounts and other easily available sources, including published evidence released by the FBI. She has no special or private sources for such information.

Authenticity of background and locale is obviously her trademark. "My research is as thorough as I can make it," she says. "I never write about a place I have not observed firsthand." She and her husband spend about three months in Europe every second year, and most of her books have been set there with strong emphasis on Austria, Switzerland, and northern Italy. She trusts implicitly the impressions that remain with her of a place and observes: "If I don't remember a place that means I'm not interested." She has a strong personal liking for maps, timetables, and guidebooks, all tools that can contribute to ultimate realism in the backgrounds of her novels.

Helen MacInnes admits to having been influenced by other writers, including George Orwell, Arthur Koestler, and Rebecca West.

Here's what she says about her working day: "I am philosophic about a working day's length. I try to get as much time in as possible, and when I am undisturbed I can work at my desk for six hours at a stretch and forget about time and meals. When interruptions occur, I just shrug, attend to them, and get back to the desk as soon as possible. I *do* love writing.

"Rewriting is constant as I go along. In my last novel, I tore up two fully written sheets for every single sheet I had in the completed manuscript. After that rewriting I check and double check and possibly reshape a page or a paragraph. The final editing generally means I go over the whole manuscript a further three or four times before my editor sees it."

She gives thanks to her Scotch parents for the discipline that has

144

characterized her life and says: "Our manners were strictly disciplined at home, our minds were severely educated in the old Scots tradition of 'give a child as much work as possible; it can learn more than you think,' and our Sundays were completely Presbyterian."

Sound Scottish common sense that, as is the following rather poetic description of her writing methods: "First you prepare the ground well, then when you plant, the whole thing grows easily, and birds come to nest in it. The characters always come if the basic structure is sound. But you must till the soil carefully first."

Ideal for emblazing on a writer's sampler.

The following novels are available in paperback.

Above Suspicion ● *Assignment in Brittany* ● *Decision at Delphi* ● *The Double Image* ● *Friends and Lovers* ● *Horizon* ● *I and My True Love* ● *Message from Malaga* ● *Neither Five nor Three* ● *North from Rome* ● *Pray for a Brave Heart* ● *Rest and Be Thankful* ● *The Salzburg Connection* ● *The Snare of the Hunter* ● *The Venetian Affair* ● *While Still We Live* ●

THE HARDEST-WORKING OF THEM ALL
JAMES A. MICHENER

In searching for words to describe this man it immediately occurs to me that James A. Michener is America's most popular author of distinction and preeminent in the whole world as an author of novels of "place." I'm referring to his three most successful novels: *Hawaii, The Source,* and *Centennial,* each of which interprets a specific locale in very elaborate detail using a place as a background as well as an integral part of the story.

There may be a subconscious explanation for this because James A. Michener is a traveler—a constant, globe-girdling, question-asking, ever-observing visitor of places. He started his restless questing early, and before he was twenty he had been in all but three states of the union. He did his traveling then by boxcar, working in carnival shows and a chautauqua company.

Somehow he found time, and had the inclination, to attend college, first Swarthmore, then St. Andrews University in Scotland. He returned to the United States to teach for about two years, first at the George School in Bucks County, Pennsylvania, next at Colorado State Teachers College and as Assistant Visiting Professor of History at Harvard University. Then came World War II. He joined the navy.

In 1945 when he was on Guadalcanal, and it was apparent that the war would soon be over, he got the stimulus that turned him to writing a book.

He noticed in this period of inactivity that the officers divided themselves into two groups, those who spent their spare time learning, and those that didn't. Most of the first group were studying something, a language or a specialty.

"The entire staff of a general hospital had been picked up and flown over to care for our wounded," he says of this situation. "The doctors had experienced days of overwork followed by weeks of tedium. In the latter periods the doctors organized voluntary study groups to further their professional competence.

"By good luck I was allowed to participate in a group that was analyzing alcoholism, and one night the leader asked me as we were breaking up, 'What are you studying, Michener?' The question stunned me, for I had been studying exactly nothing.

"I drove back through the jungle and that very night started working on something I had been toying with for some months. In a lantern-lit, mosquito-filled tin shack, I started writing *Tales of the South Pacific*."

This collection of short stories, prompted by the men and experiences he had encountered, was Michener's first book, and fate smiled upon it.

"The first story I sold to a recognized magazine was a lucky shot," he said, then he explained. "In late 1946 *The Saturday Evening Post* bought a story from my book, the then soon-to-be-published *Tales of the South Pacific*, and since the magazine could not find space for it until an early issue in 1947, publication of the book had to be delayed from 1946 to 1947. It is traditional that if a magazine purchases an excerpt from a book, magazine publication must come first. This forced postponement had a fortuitous result: the Pulitzer Prize is awarded each year to books published during the preceding calendar year, and had my inconspicuous little volume appeared in 1946 as planned, it would have been in competition with Robert Penn Warren's success, *All the King's Men*, and would not have been heard from. Instead, it was moved into 1947, not a rich year for fiction, and it copped the prize. This lucky incident made it possible for me to devote my entire efforts to free-lancing, and for it I must thank the now defunct *Saturday Evening Post*."

Possibly in part because of the publicity the Pulitzer award brought the book, Oscar Hammerstein and Josh Logan chose it as the basis for the fabled musical *South Pacific*, a box office record-setter on Broadway and one of the greatest motion pictures ever made.

What may have been the first germ of authorship planted in

Michener's consciousness as a young boy has been reported in amusing detail in the *Reader's Digest*. Briefly it is this:

It was the nine-year-old boy's responsibility to keep the lawn mowed for an elderly spinster close by his Pennsylvania home. In return she whetted his curiosity many months in advance by promising him a Christmas present in payment. "A kind of magic," she called the present-to-be.

He had hoped for a pair of ice skates, but the present turned out to be an ordinary parcel about nine inches wide, a foot long, and no more than a quarter of an inch thick.

"With great excitement," he reported, "I opened the package to find a shimmering pile of ten flimsy sheets of black paper, labeled Carbon Paper Regal Premium.

" 'What is it?' I asked.

"Aunt Laura had the presence of mind to say, 'It really is magic!' And she took two pieces of white paper, placed between them one of the black sheets from the box and, with a hard pencil, wrote my name on the upper sheet. Then removing it and the carbon paper, she handed me the second sheet, which the pencil had in no way touched.

"There was my name! It was clean and very dark and well formed and as beautiful as Christmas Day itself.

"I was enthralled! This was indeed magic—of the greatest dimension. That a pencil should write on one piece of paper and mysteriously appear on another was a miracle which was very gratifying to my childish mind. I can honestly say in that one moment, in the dark of a Christmas morning, I understood as much about printing, and the duplication of words, and the fundamental mystery of disseminating ideas as I have learned in the remaining half century of my life.

"On a white piece of paper you wrote a word and somehow it was reproduced, and you could send the copy to a friend while retaining the original for yourself. I wrote and wrote, using up whole tablets, until I had ground off the last shred of blackness from the ten sheets of carbon paper. It was the most enchanting Christmas present a boy like me could have had. It opened portals of imagination so vast that I have not yet exhausted them. It was exactly the present I needed, and it reached me at precisely that Christmas when I was best able to comprehend it.

"Having failed to get the ice skates, I am still unable to skate, a lack which has often distressed me; but because of the carbon paper I have learned something about the reproduction of words, a skill which has given me much pleasure."

In response to a series of questions asked by an interviewer,

Michener has been quite explicit as to his work habits and methods.

"I write all my books slowly, with two fingers on an old typewriter," he confessed, "and the actual task of getting the words on paper is difficult. Nothing I write is good enough to be used in first draft, not even important personal letters, so I am required to rewrite everything at least twice. Important work, like a novel, must be written over and over again, up to six or seven times. For example, *Hawaii* went very slowly and needed constant revision. Since the final version contained about 500,000 words, and since I wrote it all many times, I had to type, in my painstaking fashion, about 3,000,000 words."

"How many research books did you consult?" he was asked.

"Several thousand. When I started the actual writing, there were about five hundred that I kept in my office."

"How many personal interviews?"

"About two hundred. Each two or three hours long."

"Did you write much that you were unable to use?"

"I had to throw away about half a million words."

"Would you have the energy to undertake such a task again?" he was asked.

"I would always like to be engaged in such tasks," was the reply, and he offers in fuller explanation: "Young people, especially those in college who should know better, frequently fail to realize that men and women who wish to accomplish anything must apply themselves to tasks of tremendous magnitude. A new vaccine may take years to perfect. A Broadway play is never written, cast, and produced in a week.

"The good work of the world is accomplished principally by people who dedicate themselves unstintingly to the big job at hand. Weeks, months, years pass, but the good workman knows that he is gambling on an ultimate achievement which cannot be measured in time spent. Responsible men and women leap to the challenge of jobs that require enormous dedication and years to fulfill—as does book writing—and are happiest when they are so involved."

If it is your dream to have a paneled den before you write that book, you will be interested in this author's comments about his working conditions and habits. The first concerns *Hawaii*.

"I holed up in a bare-wall no-telephone Waikiki room and stuck at my typewriter every morning for eighteen months. Seven days a week I wrestled with the words that would not come, with ideas that refused to jell. When I broke a tooth, I told the dentist I would have to see him at night."

The following concerns his writing in remote areas, where hotel rooms were not available:

"When I started to write, often under incredibly difficult circumstances, I sought only a large flat space on which to arrange my papers. One of the best working surfaces I ever used was an unfinished door propped up on cement blocks. This supplies a big solid expanse on which to spread papers. I have written three of my novels on such a door. I have written in the tropics, in the arctic, with noise on every side, and in various paradises like Samoa and Ceylon, but the places I remember with most affection were the quiet bare rooms without much view."

When young college-age students have asked Michener how they could best prepare themselves for a writing career outside the world of fiction, he has invariably told them: "If I were a young man with writing talent and wanted to make a major contribution, I would turn my attention to some area of the world about which America knows little, and I would school myself to be an expert in that field. I'd study the language, the religion, the history, the geography, and the contemporary politics and literature. After about eight or ten years I'd be in a position to make a positive contribution."

And when asked what region of the world he would suggest, he has said, with great foresight, "Islam. It's bound to become a major world problem and will be with us for the next fifty years. Learn Arabic. Learn the religion. And travel in Muslim countries whenever you can.

"My second choice has been Africa, my third South America."

It was his first book, *Tales of the South Pacific*, that also got his second publication in a national magazine. You will remember the *Post* took one chapter, and it was the *Reader's Digest* that took another. This led to a very close relationship between Michener and the *Digest* editors and subsequent publication of many pieces in the *Digest*. These pieces and detailed explanations of how each happened to be written form the content of a most interesting book, *A Michener Miscellany*, a Reader's Digest Press Book, available through Random House.

It is in that book, where he has published words of encouragement for would-be writers, that he says, "The rules seem to be these: If you have written a successful novel, publishers invite you to write short stories. If you have written some good short stories, publishers want you to write a novel. But nobody wants anything until you have already proved yourself by being published somewhere else.

Cutting that Gordian knot is as difficult now as it was in 1750, and as essential. You cut it by writing and writing and writing and doing anything possible to find any publisher anywhere."

As you have gone along with me on these pages, you have read how important all authors, with hardly an exception, consider rewriting and final preparation of the manuscript. The following, written by James A. Michener and originally published in *Publishers Weekly*, will give you an insight into a working arrangement between Michener and his editor, Albert Erskine, that is so total as to be unique. It is further proof, also, that a true writer is never satisfied until he believes he has achieved his best:

Few writers can have profited so much from editorial assistance as I have from working with Albert Erskine of Random House. I write long books, complex ones, and I take a long time doing so, and I doubt that I could have seen them through to completion without the assistance of a professional overseer. Erskine has been ideal.

In planning a book I tell him only briefly what I am considering. I do not look to him for guidance in plotting, in characterization or in emphasis on ideas. That's my job. Nor do I allow him to see segments as the work progresses. I work severely alone and show my work to no one, for only I can make the necessary decisions.

But once the work is completed to my satisfaction—after about two years of intense preoccupation—I want all the help I can get. I therefore turn the manuscript over to Erskine, who is a brilliant man intellectually and a perceptive one artistically, and ask him to identify everything that's wrong. He spends a long time at this preliminary study, then calls me into his office with a small notebook filled with objections and suggestions.

He does not say, as happens so often in motion picture accounts of writing and editing, "That character must go," or "The whole middle section is out." I would not accept such judgments.

What he does do is point with devilish accuracy at points where I have gone wrong; at interior contradictions, at sloppy motivations for specific acts, at solecisms, at words I have misused because I haven't known their classical derivations, at lack of balance in sentences, at adverbs that might work better if placed elsewhere or best if dropped. In other words, Albert Erskine is an educated man with one hell of a good eye, which is all-important.

I have written elsewhere of my battle with him over the word "transpire," which he would not admit, only to find that major dictionaries were using the word in its new connotation and citing me as the authority. I could have recited a dozen other linguistic adventures, all growing out of his erudition.

We spend about three weeks on this part of the review, with me sitting at his desk six or seven hours a day, battling over every sentence of the book. Over the weekends I return home with a score of assignments, on which I slave prior to the next meeting. At the end of this period I have about a month's work ahead of me, rewriting sections that didn't come off the first time.

We then go over the entire manuscript again, not line by line this time, but hitting all parts that were questioned the first time. We edit and rewrite and perfect single sentences and redraft—he giving the criticisms, I doing the work—and after a couple of months the manuscript is ready to be turned over to Erskine's proofreading wizard, Miss Bert Krantz, who over a period of two months catches absolutely bizarre errors that had slipped by Erskine and me. Again I work for three or four weeks, hours each day, rewriting and perfecting lines.

We now send the manuscript to the typesetter, after which Erskine and I repeat the process, taking a couple of months to read every word and to fight over obscurities. The galleys then go to Bert Krantz, who reads them all two or three times and sits with me again for hours, arguing over words and meanings. I do a lot of rewriting in galley, after which we go to page proof.

Again Erskine and Krantz and I fight for clarity, redoing whole pages if necessary. When we are finished and have made all corrections, revised pages then go to a completely fresh reader who looks with jaundiced eye at everything we've done and finds her own set of contradictions, which we correct agonizingly, because we are now in pages. But she catches things none of us would ever have suspected and the book is better for her attention.

In the meantime Erskine has been attending to the artwork for the book, the cover, the flap copy, the presentation to the Random House salesmen, the other odd jobs related to publishing a book —tedious to me but essential to any book. I allow him to make all such decisions because I am not interested in them. Finally, the book appears.

This is a tedious process. I work endlessly upon it. As you can see, it requires me to read the manuscript and galleys about twenty-five times, and there is little that has been written in this world that is worth reading that often except the Gettysburg Address and the Twenty-third Psalm. The process requires my presence in Erskine's office for about four months, off and on, and reading until my eyes weaken. It is a heavy burden on Erskine and perhaps he does more work than necessary.

But out of this has come a series of books which have enjoyed wide acceptance throughout the world. I have worked in many different fields and kept my imaginative life alive. At sixty-five I am burgeoning with ideas for additional books. And I have had to be ashamed of little that I have written. For these good results I must thank Erskine for the creative role he played.

I am aware that not all writers would want this kind of association with their editors. I am increasingly aware that the new-style conglomerate publisher would not want his editors to waste so much time on one writer. I am sorrowfully aware that many editors would not have the intellectual capability to work with a writer as Erskine has worked with me. But in our case the working pattern has proved remarkably productive, and if, when I wanted this kind of editor, Bennett Cerf had not had Erskine at hand I would have looked elsewhere until I found someone like him. For I knew clearly what I needed.

These closing facts are all important. I have never asked Erskine to get me theater tickets. I don't want him to meet me at the boat when I come home with a manuscript. I don't ask him to supervise my personal life. I would look at him blankly if he said, "What you ought to write next is another book about the South Pacific." And I have never felt that I could get much spiritual help out of him if I suddenly started to go dry. Those are all my problems, and I do not look to him for their solution. What I want from him is editorial help, something he is admirably prepared to supply.

His major attraction for me, however, is that he likes Italian and Chinese food, my favorites.

The following books by James A. Michener are available in paper-back:

The Bridge at Andau ● *The Bridges at Toko-Ri* ● *Caravans* ● *The Drifters* ● *Fires of Spring* ● *Hawaii* ● *Iberia: Spanish Travels and Reflections* ● *Kent State: What Happened and Why* ● *Rascals in Paradise* ● *Return to Paradise* ● *Sayonara* ● *The Source* ● *Tales of the South Pacific* ● *A Michener Miscellany, 1950–1970* ● *Centennial* ● *Sports in America* ●

A NOVELIST OF ENERGY, INTEGRITY, DEDICATION
JOYCE CAROL OATES

While still in her early thirties Ms. Oates is recognized universally as an important and serious novelist, yet the novels she has written escape the turgidness that afflicts so much of what is called "serious" or "literary" in the world of writing.

She is a slender, willowy woman, her beauty that of the patrician daughter of a noble Byzantine family, and giving no hint of the stamina and dedication that has produced a flood of novels, poems, essays, plays, and short stories. She has written a total of ten novels to date, five of them in the last ten years. Her novel *A Garden of Earthly Delights* was nominated for the National Fiction Award, and her book *Them* won that award. She won a Guggenheim Fellowship in 1967–68. Her short stories have been widely anthologized, and she was first prize winner of the O. Henry Prize Awards in 1967. Her stories have been frequently included, too, in *Best American Short Stories*.

Today Ms. Oates is Professor of English at the University of Windsor, Ontario, where her husband, Raymond Smith, also teaches. They met and married while both were doing graduate work at the University of Wisconsin. Her earlier university work had been done at Syracuse University. "She was the most brilliant student we ever had here," stated Donald A. Dike, Professor of English, to whom her book *With Shuddering Fall* is dedicated. "About once a term she'd drop a 400-page novel on my desk." In recent years her rapid production of books has caused some concern among critics that she may be producing too much.

Perhaps these critics would be mollified with a statement in a recent letter to me about her working habits: "I have always written quickly, . . . now I am working slowly, working out well in advance what each chapter (of my new novel) will be. Then I intend to rewrite it all. I am doing this experimentally since it is somewhat against my nature, but I want to try other methods of writing, other techniques. This novel, *How Lucien Florey Came To Be Born*, will probably take many years to complete."

Joyce Carol Oates is a novelist in the pristine sense. She has taken the novel back to its root meaning—"news." Her goal is to mirror life as it is today, as she knows it and observes it. Because of this devotion to truth, her books contain and reflect violence and such ugliness as is woefully present in our time. Many who know her, and some critics, find it difficult to equate the very serene young woman who has a timid demeanor and little-girl voice with the rape, murders, incest, and tragedy that populate her novels. Although she grew up on a farm and thus knows the reality of animals and humans living close to the soil, it would seem, these people say, she would be insulated from the cruelties and even perversions of life today, yet these are important elements in her writing.

In her novel *Wonderland*, for instance, a young man survives the slaughter of his whole family by his father, only to fall into an equally nightmarish life with a foster father, certainly far from anything the author experienced or personally observed.

Her interesting explanation is that the germ for this, probably her most impressive novel, came from a newspaper item. "I read it years ago," she said. "It took a very long time for this to work itself through my imagination and to emerge into consciousness, and the entire process is unknown to me. But the important thing, for me, is that the novel's basis is a real event; that it happened in the world 'out there' and not in my head."

All of her fiction comes from reality—incidents she may pick up anywhere—and she acknowledges that the germ of her novel *Them* came from the experiences and memories of one of her students.

As a teacher of creative writing Ms. Oates is consciously dedicated to helping others write. She loves teaching and is very good at it. "I wish it would never end," says one student of her course in contemporary literature.

She admits to being personally and deeply concerned with the phenomenon of "creativity," and calls it "one of the most mysterious of all human endeavors."

She states further that in her opinion the process of creating cannot be explained in rational or scientific terms, but that "writers can share with one another their knowledge of how the process can be stimulated and formalized."

A most interesting and tenable theory advanced by her is the belief that happiness by the individual results in a rush of creative activity.

"I firmly believe," she explains, "that mankind is so instinctively, unconsciously involved with the survival and growth of the species that when an individual attempts to live selfishly, he will either fail or fall into despair. Only when men are connected to large, universal goals are they really happy—and one result of their happiness is a rush of creative activity."

Ms. Oates has been widely quoted concerning her belief that "the average person is deeper, more talented, and more intelligent that he probably believes. He is," she insists, "transformable—even overnight. Exhaustion and fatigue are mainly psychological; if man is faced with a new challenge he can summon up an enormous reservoir of energy."

As a serious author concerned with the novel as an art form, she has this to say about the author as an artist: "Anyone who is writing to make money is deluding himself; he is writing for other and deeper reasons, reasons he cannot explain. But as long as he believes that he is writing for money or for prestige, he will write in a falsifying way, manufacturing emotions in conformity with emotions he sees in others; and yet his own life is filled with enough drama to constitute any number of novels. When one writes about his true subject, in contrast to the false subject, he really has no difficulty with writing."

To writers who find themselves blocked she offers: "Any writer who has difficulty in writing is probably not onto his true subject, but wasting time with false, petty goals; as soon as you connect with your subject you will write."

In reply to my query regarding her writing habits, she has supplied the following:

On a practical level I can offer only a few general advisory words, which may be too personal for broader application.

My "ideas" come to me partly out of the world (I scan newspapers often) and partly out of my own life. They seem to sink into unconsciousness, sometimes for a long period of time, and are drawn out again by some stray reminder in my daily life (in the case of *Wonderland*, I came across a number of similar news items—dealing with the murder-suicide tragedy, eerily common in our country, in which a father kills his entire family and then himself).

Then a long process of "dreaming through" takes place, in which I think about the entire novel—living through various scenes, hearing or inventing dialogue, walking around with my characters in my head for months; only when the process is completed can I begin to write, and I can't hurry the process. I can assign to myself occasional tasks—how to manage a certain scene, how to dramatize the relationship of one character to another—before going to sleep at night, and sometimes by morning I have figured out the problem —sometimes—this might work about half the time. But I never despair or become impatient; it is simply a matter of waiting until the entire book is thought out.

After this strange, uncanny, intuitive stage of a novel is more or less completed in my mind, I write the first draft. I usually write very quickly, chapter by chapter, though I try to alternate work on a novel with shorter pieces—stories, articles, or reviews—in order to keep some objectivity.

I always know exactly how the novel will end, even the wording of the final paragraph. I always know exactly the crucial scenes, the dialogue, even the way my characters look, though I may not describe them in that much detail. But as I write this first draft, I often discover new, small things about my characters, and allow any workable rearrangements in. This year, spent in London, I wrote a rather long novel titled *Do With Me What You Will*, which is a complex narrative dealing with the law—the legal profession in America—but concentrating on two individuals who happen to be lovers, and who are married and "thinking back" over the circumstances of their having met and fallen in love; it involved many exasperating problems, but as long as I waited patiently, the narrative always straightened out and the characters asserted themselves in accordance with their own integrity.

After the first draft is finished, I put it aside temporarily and work on other things. Then when I feel the time has come for me to really formalize it, I begin the second and final draft—and this part of the process is strangely enough the most enjoyable of all. I cut each chapter drastically, seeing as objectively as possible what can be eliminated or shortened (my manuscripts would be very long, sometimes twice as long, if I didn't cut so severely), trying to read the work as if from another part of myself, or from the point of view of another person. Though the original, spontaneous part of writing can be very exciting, the real reward for me at least is this third and most conscious, most "intellectual" organization of material. Man is a problem-solving animal and the organizing of vast subjects must give pleasure, evidently; nothing seems to me to involve more intellectual effort than the organizing of a big novel, and I cannot imagine anything more rewarding.

The following books of Joyce Carol Oates are in paperback:
By the North Gate ● *Do With Me What You Will* ● *Expensive People* ● *A Garden of Earthly Delights* ● *Marriages and Infidelities* ● *Them* ● *Upon the Sweeping Flood* ● *Wheel of Love* ● *With Shuddering Fall* ● *Wonderland* ● *The Edge of Impossibility: Tragic Forms of Literature* ● *Love and Its Derangements and Other Poems* ● *Where Are You Going, Where Have You Been: Stories of Young America* ● *The Assassins* ●

MR. "POSITIVE THINKING"
NORMAN VINCENT PEALE

The Reverend Norman Vincent Peale is today's leading author of inspirational books. To him goes all credit for popularizing the magic phrase "positive thinking," as introduced in what is his best-known book and biggest best-seller, *The Power of Positive Thinking*.

He is famous as an author and public speaker, one who is almost constantly on tour, speaking at universities, national conventions, large industrial gatherings, and wherever men and women can be reached with his inspiring messages. But his first fame is as a minister, pastor of New York's Marble Collegiate Church. His sermons on radio and television have made him America's best-known religious voice.

Although the greatest emphasis in this book has been on the writing of novels and the authors of novels, I would like to repeat that the factual book, the nonfiction category, actually outsells the works of fiction. And again, more nonfiction books are published. Also, the whole area of factual writing is one in which more people are quickly qualified to write than in the more esoteric field of the novel. There is a hunger everywhere among readers for facts that are useful or of interest to them; facts of every sort: from information concerning a favorite hobby to unusual true stories, such as exposé books on the Mafia, how-to-do books, books on personal experiences, textbooks, and so on. The subject matter is limitless, and if your desire is to write a factual book you could have no better instructor than this expert in the field.

Q. What in your background contributed to your becoming an author? What were the circumstances that led to your first book and how did it get published?

A. I went to New York to Marble Collegiate Church as minister in 1932. At that time we were at the bottom of the Great Depression. I had come from a university pulpit in New York State where the intellectual atmosphere was strong, and I guess my sermons there reflected that emphasis to a certain extent. But when I came to New York, I found people up against the practical necessities of life, such as a man who had lost his job or was frightened because of the alarming economic conditions. It was really a sad time. So I began to give talks in the church—practical talks—on How do you handle fear? How do you stop waking up in the middle of the night with palpitations of the heart when suffering from

157

anxiety? People began to come to talk to me and ask for personal help.

One day as I walked on lower Fifth Avenue near the church, I met John W. Longdale, an old friend, who was editor of the Abingdon Press, the publishing house.

"Norman," he said, "I've been hearing of the kind of talks you're giving to people who are having difficulties at this time. Why don't you write a book?"

"Well," I replied, "I've thought of it, but I don't know whether I could do it or not. I've never tried to write a book."

"Why don't you use the material in your talks?" he asked. "Don't put it in sermon form, but put it in chapter form under headings, and prepare a manuscript and bring it down and let me see it."

He also told me that the only way in the world you can ever write a book—you can think about it, you can discuss it, you can plan it, but the only way you can write a book is to sit down with a blank piece of paper and put down one word. Then you follow with a second word and a third word and after a while you've got 1,000 words. And then you are on your way.

I wrote this little book after much struggle. It wasn't more than 25,000 words altogether, if that. It was called *The New Art of Living*. To my surprise it had a very good sale. Then we tried another. I had titled it *You Can Win Over Anything*, or any obstacle, or something like that. He dropped the last words and made it *You Can Win*. I always thought it was a mistake. I didn't think that title was so good. But that book had a good sale, too.

So I started writing a long string of books designed to help people meet the problems of life. That's how I got started at it.

Q. What is your advice to those who want to write but don't know how to get started?

A. It's hard work. I get manuscripts or several chapters from people who want to write books. In many cases, they just do not know how to go about it. They do not put it together properly. They do not build an orderly outline. They seem lacking in the ability of getting the interest of the reader with the opening paragraphs, the attention getters, and so forth.

They do not dramatize their material. You've got to make it so it attracts and holds the readers' interest. Sustained interest is a hard thing to achieve. Even the brightest person in the world can't hold to the same subject for too long a time.

One thing that I think is a mistake is that so many people who try to write are constantly striving for some kind of literary effect. It seems to me that the way to write is to know what you want to say, then say it in the simplest and most interesting way possible. Tell your story and then end it, as a newspaper editor once told me. He took a piece of paper and put down what I construed to be a dot. "What is that?" he asked. "It's a dot," I said. "No," he replied, "that is a period. That is the greatest literary device known to man. Write up to the period. Do not run over it." In other words, do not be wordy.

You certainly must have something constructive to say. You must have a message. If you do have it, and you really feel it, and are enthusiastic about it, and indeed, are wrapped up in it, then if you put it down in a simple, direct fashion, you are communicating. I think writing that is any good has to have the communication element in it. You have to talk to your reader in terms that he can comprehend.

Q. What are your writing habits? Where do you write? What time of day?

A. I can do much better in the morning. I'm fresher. I can stick at it for a longer period of time, and my energies seem to be at a maximum. So, what I like to do when I'm really going to do a writing job, such as writing a book, is to get out of bed at six o'clock, get dressed, have breakfast, and get everything out of the way so I can start working at seven o'clock.

I write in longhand. In fact, I write every single word myself with a pencil. I use plain white paper and have perhaps a couple dozen pencils lined up, all sharpened. I write with one until it is worn down and then throw it aside and write with another, and finally I pick them all up, sharpen them again, and then start wearing them down again. I sharpen them myself with an electric sharpener.

The reason I do not dictate is that I found out when dictating I tended to be too wordy and the copy required so much editing that it was a time consumer and an extra burden. If you write by hand with a pencil it has to be at a slower pace, and I think you produce a much better sentence. I do a lot of crossing out, I must say. I don't stop to erase. I cross out and go on.

After I've written two to three thousand words I go through the penciled copy and correct it and mark it up. Sometimes it looks pretty terrible. Then, when I can't read it any more myself, because it is so marked up, I have it typed. I then go over the typed copy once;

I may take out some material or put more in. The copy turns out to be fairly clean after the first typing, as a rule, because the major revision has been in the penciled work.

So, first it is in pencil, then it is in typewriter, then it is in typewriter again, and that presumably is the final copy that goes to the editor.

I can work from 7:00 A.M. to noon. That is about five hours. Once in a while during those five hours, if I am at our farm in Pawling, I go out and walk around the house or down to the gate, maybe a couple of times during the five hours, or just stroll around the room. One gets tired of sitting.

But once I get going, I can keep writing strenuously until I either finish the job or until lunchtime.

I do a lot of research. For example, I am writing a book right now. I've got folders with chapter titles on them. Everything that I think will go into each chapter is in a folder. If I'm going to work tomorrow morning, this afternoon or tonight I will go over the material in tomorrow's folder, letting it sort of soak into my consciousness overnight. Then I organize it, putting facts down in one, two, three fashion, as the material falls naturally into place. That way I have it systematically lined up. When I start the actual writing, I find that I use perhaps only about half the material that was in the folder, because I seldom run a chapter over five thousand words.

If there is material left over from the chapter I have blocked out, I look through the succeeding chapter folders to see if any of the material left over would fit into them. This is a kind of outlining process, but I do not put down "point one," "point two," "subdivision a," or anything like that.

I find that when you get to writing, if you have all the material in your mind, it starts to fall into place—if you are going well. Now, if you are not going well, it may not fall into place so easily. Then you might as well wait until you feel you can get the rhythm flowing again. I was reading recently about Pearl Buck, who found that as she got older she could not work as long. She discovered that when her energy began to wane, her writing did not flow quite so well. That, she says, is the time to quit. If you force yourself to go on, your writing loses impact.

I am fortunate in being able to write anywhere I may be. I have done much writing in hotel rooms. If I can get a quiet room and not be bothered by telephones, I can do a lot of work. I have even written on airplanes. But I think I work best in our farmhouse on Quaker Hill in Pawling, if I have someone to answer the phone. The phone is a nuisance; it breaks your line of thought and gets you involved in other matters.

Q. Has writing become easier for you with each book?

A. I really think it gets a little easier. Pearl Buck, again, said she had that experience. She felt that may have been because she had had more experience and had matured and ideas flowed from her; she had a greater inner reservoir of material. I feel somewhat the same way.

I met a man on a train years ago. He was a newspaperman from upstate New York, with the Gannett newspapers. He took me to task because I was writing with a nice long fresh pencil. He said the only kind of pencil to work with is one that has been worn down so you can put it in a vest pocket. He found my pencils to be "too high class!"

Q. How long does it take you to write a book?

A. I had a peculiar experience with *The Power of Positive Thinking*. I started it and then I showed it to a friend who was in the publishing business. He said, "It is no good," so I put it away for nearly a year. Then I got it out and started over. So that book took me about a year and a half.

It was much different with a later book called *A Tough-Minded Optimist*. I went to Switzerland, and lived in a mountain chalet. There in two month's time I wrote half of it, because I worked constantly. I did nothing else, only that book. The current one I'm working on I started writing in late February in Philadelphia in a hotel, and now it is April and I've finished five chapters. That is a month and a half for five chapters. I've promised to finish it by September 1, and believe I can make the deadline.

The title? I haven't got a title. I've written down several. First I was going to call it *You Can Overcome Any Problem*, or *You Can Handle Any Problem*. But it isn't so much about problems. It *is* but it *isn't*. So then I began to realize I was really writing about how wonderful people are. So then I thought I might call it *People Are Terrific!* Then I got another title, *Take a New Look at the Impossible*. But I don't like that either.

The method I have usually used is to write the book first. Then in reading it over, the title emerges from the text. When you write a book, you are saying something in 65,000 words, so there is always inherent in the copy the phrase that best describes what you are saying.

But I haven't always been lucky with titles. It might be easier to have a title before you begin, because then you could weave it into the text. I always do have a theme, however. In this case the theme is: believe in yourself. There are chapter titles such as "It's Always Too Soon to Quit," "Uptight, Tense, Relax," "What Are You Afraid Of?" and so forth. I quote Emerson who said that self-trust is the first secret of success. It's a build-up kind of book, so that if you read it, you ought to be built-up.

Q. How is your spelling?

A. My spelling is not very good, but I've got secretaries who know how to spell. I don't allow myself to get hung up with spelling. I just write a word the best I can and the secretaries correct it if need be. I'd get hung up if I stopped writing to check spelling.

Q. What is the most difficult thing about writing—for you?

A. Getting started on the first chapter. I once asked a great writer what he thought the secret of writing was. "Well," he said, "it's the long, continued application of the seat of the pants to a chair." In other words, sitability.

He said he once sat down to prepare an editorial and wrote: "It is perfectly obvious . . ." Then he sat there for half an hour trying to figure out what was obvious.

It's getting started—like opening a bottle of olives. You get the first olive out of the bottle and the rest come out easily.

As for writing style, I personally like the short sentence and the short paragraph. You must have flow in writing. If writing is stilted, you don't get a rhythmic flow. A reader should be carried along, progressing from one thought to another. Sentences should march along like soldiers going somewhere in direct, orderly fashion.

Q. Do you have any favorite writers who have influenced you?

A. I would say that newspaper writers, good ones, reporters, have influenced me. I have always admired the succinct style, short sentences, short words. In other words, in making a statement I reach for the shortest word I can find to say the thing that I want to say.

So wherever I've found newspaper writers such as those who write for the New York *Daily News,* for example, I find a great economy of words. Other writers have influenced me, but more on the basis of content rather than writing style.

162

Q. What is your advice to someone who wants to write a book?

A. Write it! Get into it. Love it. Try to help the reader handle life more effectively.

Following are the author's books in paperback:
The Amazing Results of Positive Thinking ● *Enthusiasm Makes the Difference* ● *A Guide to Confident Living* ● *The New Art of Living* ● *The Power of Positive Thinking* ● *Sin, Sex and Self-Control* ● *Stay Alive All Your Life* ● *The Tough-Minded Optimist* ●

HER EVERY NOVEL
A BEST-SELLER
MARY STEWART

Two of this author's recent novels, *The Crystal Cave* and *The Hollow Hills*, are great best-sellers and unique historical novels of literary excellence; the "history" they reflect is the King Arthur legend and the life of Merlin. Both books became No. 1 in sales on the most important index of book sales in the United States, that of *The New York Times*.

These two books were preceded over an eighteen-year span by eleven more easily defined, romantic suspense novels, each laid in an exotic setting with which the author was personally familiar.

A quick index to her popularity is the fact that more than 20 million copies of her books have been printed in Fawcett paperback, with many thousand more hardcover copies in print with William Morrow in the United States and with Hodder-Stoughton in England. She is reprinted in virtually all languages.

Q. What is the trigger that starts you planning a novel?
A. A place which has had a powerful impact on my senses and imagination usually suggests a story line to me, a place where I can put my characters and let their reactions to that place work themselves into a situation or a plot. I used to think it was chance that led me into this way of writing. Now, almost without realizing it, I have come to have the reputation of setting my stories in exotic places—Avignon, Skye, Savoy, Corfu—and using these settings as not just background but almost as the "first character" in a book. When I wrote my first book, I launched myself into this pattern. It seemed natural, in that icy winter when my impulsion to write

163

finally outweighed even my diffidence in starting, to choose the hottest and most exciting place I had then been to—Provence, a French resort city. The book was *Madam, Will You Talk?* I found, in the writing of the book, that the tough, strange, romantic setting exactly suited the kind of thing I wanted to write. It did, in fact, dictate its own kind of plot.

Q. You have been called "a born storyteller." Do you agree?

A. I do agree and I hope this does not indicate a lack of modesty. As far back as I can remember storytelling came naturally to me. I couldn't help it. Others may be good at golf or mathematics; I can tell stories and bring fictional people and places to life. I came to writing because it seemed the obvious thing to do with my life; and others who have this gift seem to move naturally into writing. My storywriting started when I was a child. I can remember sitting on the attic floor with my toys around me, writing stories about them with self-made illustrations. I had only three toys: a horse, an elephant, and a cat, the play kind, of course. Throughout my childhood I read widely and avidly and continued writing stories for myself: poems and tales of wonder and adventure.

Then, as I got older, work came and life crowded in. I wrote a good deal of poetry while I was teaching at the university, but it was sometime later, after marriage and the tragedy of losing a first child, that I came again to storywriting. The first thing I wrote was a sort of summary of all those childhood tales. It was a long story for children called *The Enchanted Journey*. It was written not so much for children as for me and the child I had been. I certainly made no concessions to immaturity. So, you might say I came to the writing of novels via poetry and literature and the myth or folktale.

I am country bred, with a deep interest in natural history, and a passion for ancient history and folklore. So I find that my kind of imagination quickens most readily in beautiful places where legend and history add an extra light of excitement to the kind of life that is lived today.

Q. Was the writing of your first novel easy?

A. No. It wasn't easy, and no writer worth his salt ever found it easy or ever will. I'm sure there is something heartening and helpful about writers sharing their community of experience, and the one I would emphasize, and find all writers agree on, is that writing is hard work, very hard work; and, perhaps for that reason, can be very rewarding.

Q. How long did it take to write your first novel?

A. It took me about two years, and it never once occurred to me in that time that it might be publishable. I wrote it for myself. It was my husband who made me send it away, with the (very Scottish) encouragement that: "It might as well be out of the house as in it." While it was out of the house I started straightaway on another, *Thunder on the Right.* I was still, of course, doing my own housework, all the gardening, lecturing on literature five days a week at the University, and spending a lot of evenings correcting essays or working with the University Dramatic Society. On Christmas Eve, 1953, Hodder and Stoughton sent me a contract for that first novel, *Madam, Will You Talk?* and we were off.

Q. Did you get editorial help from your publisher?

A. The publisher's guidance about length, construction, and various technical points in my first novel made me realize that *Thunder on the Right* in its unlicked form would never do, so I put it aside for rewriting, and wrote another, *Wildfire at Midnight.* Then I rewrote *Thunder on the Right.* I had used a different approach for it—third person instead of first—but found it awkward, so from *Wildfire* on I kept to the first person narrative form.

Q. Were your books successful from the first?

A. It is very satisfying that they have all been best-sellers, but even if they hadn't been I doubt if my publishers could have stopped me from writing if they had wanted to. There was a lot of territory still unexplored.

Then in the autumn of 1956 my husband was appointed Regius Professor in Geology in Edinburgh University. We were lucky in our house-hunting—a smallish, easily run, stone-built house in southwest Edinburgh, barely a couple of miles from open country and the Pentland Hills. The garden was ideal—small, walled, and with some well-grown blossoming trees, and not much else except possibilities. After ten years it is a very pretty garden indeed. Once settled in Edinburgh, I decided (I was halfway through *Nine Coaches Waiting*) that I must give up university work and now give all my time to writing.

Q. What are your working conditions?

A. For the past several years I have employed a part-time secretary to help with my heavy and ever-growing correspondence, and to clear the decks to let me get some writing time to myself. I still

165

do my own housekeeping and cooking; I have to have solitude to write in, and couldn't settle to work with anyone else in the house.

Q. What is your writing procedure?
A. I keep regular hours daily; a writer has no one else to force her to punch a clock, and so self-discipline is very necessary. The number of hours varies according to the stage the current book is at. The early or most difficult stages are done in shorter bursts—six hours' writing or two thousand words per day, whichever target is reached first. Of course if it goes well, I go on as long as I can. Towards the end of a book it is so alive and all-consuming for me that I find it hard to stop writing, and then the self-discipline has to be imposed to make me put writing aside and attend to the chores. My mornings are spent on whatever domestic chores have to be done, on correspondence, and on such "casual" writing as crops up—articles and so on. My secretary works with me from 9:30 til 1:00 P.M. I use a variety of techniques, whichever is convenient—typing, writing, using a dictating machine, or dictating "live"—though this last is only for letters.

From 1:00 P.M. onwards I write, stopping at 7:00 P.M. to prepare dinner. I may go on writing if I've been interrupted before (a woman writing in her own home is very vulnerable to interruption) or if the wheels are turning well, and I don't want to stop.

Each book is completely written three times and then given a polish and overhaul.

Working from chapter synopsis, family trees, maps, notes of ideas, and "big scenes" previously prepared, I half-write, half-dictate a draft. It takes about three or four months. It gives me a rough working outline of the novel, and by the end of it the scenes are set in my head and the people have got rounded out into reality. If I come across snags or discrepancies or suddenly have ideas that blow some previous idea sky-high, I simply carry on and develop it "live" as it comes. I skip descriptions, which are incredibly difficult, and wing through conversations, which are worse. Action and movement are easy. Frequently I never retouch them.

The real writing is slow and painful, sometimes a day or more over a paragraph. I start by combing the first draft through and listing every alteration. Then I rewrite, chapter by chapter. It takes about six months. Then I leave it aside for at least three weeks without looking at it, while I read up and research things I found I needed to know but didn't want to stop for.

This is where the book is cut, shaped, tightened up, discrepancies ironed out; each character taken out and looked at as an individual so that actions and speech are consistent. Details of place are checked with maps, photographs, and so on. Sometimes even at this stage a new idea is written in, or a mistake is found which breaks right across some piece of structure and is a real job to put right.

Finally, I have fun matching quotations to the chapter headings and adding the polish here and there; and then starting to worry myself stupid because the book isn't good enough and not what I'd originally set out to do.

Mary Stewart's novels printed in paperback are:
Airs Above the Ground ● *The Crystal Cave* ● *The Gabriel Hounds* ● *The Hollow Hills* ● *The Ivy Tree* ● *Madam, Will You Talk?* ● *The Moon-Spinners* ● *My Brother Michael* ● *Nine Coaches Waiting* ● *This Rough Magic* ● *Thunder on the Right* ● *Wildfire at Midnight* ●

A UNIQUE FORMULA FOR WRITING SUCCESS
JOHN TOLAND

John Toland may be best known for his more than one-thousand-page book, *Adolf Hitler*, although he won a Pulitzer Prize for *The Rising Sun*. Before that there were *The Last 100 Days*, *The Dillinger Days*, *But Not in Shame*, *Battle: The Story of the Bulge* and *Ships in the Sky*—every book successful and every book nonfiction.

Unlike the case of other authors in this section, I did not publish any of Mr. Toland's books in paperback, but his first published factual story, a short piece in *Cavalier*, a Fawcett magazine, was under my responsibility as editorial director of the company. I am including Mr. Toland in this section on that thin excuse because John Toland's peculiar experiences in gaining success as a writer may be of exceptional value to other writers. For it is a fact that in spite of his now imposing record of success, John Toland had an even longer record of failure as a writer. In his dramatic, satisfying experience of turning failure into triumph there may be meaningful encouragement, possibly even a success pattern for others to follow.

Here is his record of failure: From the time John Toland started writing for publication he produced six novels. None was published. He wrote twenty-five completed plays. None was produced. He wrote more than one hundred short stories before one was published. John Toland was forty-two years old when his first book was published. It was not until after some twenty years of diligent

167

writing and rewriting that he stumbled upon, or had thrust upon him, the one discovery that enabled him to become a success as an author of books.

John's ambition to be a writer was first awakened at age fourteen when his father, a concert singer and gregarious man, brought Porter Emerson Browne, a playwright, to live in the family home. Browne's most famous play was *The Badman.* He was an entertaining, happy, chubby, romantic world traveler and raconteur who had been in China with war lords and in Mexico with Pancho Villa. He spent hours, weeks and months, conversing with the adulating young boy, already in love with the world of books. So profound was the playwright's influence that young Toland decided, as a teenager, to become a playwright. He never lost track of this goal throughout his self-won schooling.

There was not much money in the Toland household. "We were poor, but never hungry," is the way the author characterizes his early boyhood. John became one of the few students to work his way through the socially prominent prep school, Exeter. He paid his way with money earned during summer vacations when he worked as a janitor in a tire factory, and by serving, during the school terms, as a waiter in the school dining room. From Exeter he went to Williams College where he developed an interest in the novel and proved his interest by writing one complete novel during each of the four years he attended the college, also managing to earn money in such diverse ways as clerking in a book store, running a typing service, waiting on table and rising to the status of headwaiter. While at Williams, and later at Yale School of the Drama, he wrote the twenty-five plays that were never produced.

After Yale there followed several years of writing short stories, mostly about his experiences while riding freight trains around the Depression-mired country, and none of the stories found a publisher.

Then, Pearl Harbor, and John Toland enlisted in the Air Force, serving two hitches. He went in as an enlisted man in 1942, served four years, stayed out a year, was invited back in 1947, and came out a captain.

Between army services, and after, he worked at a variety of jobs, including owning a gift shop that went broke, selling, and attempting to write short fiction stories for magazines. How did he live during these years? His answer: "Mostly on what I saved from my Army salary, but miserably!"

He did sell a short science fiction magazine story entitled *Watercure* for very little money, several more science fiction stories, also for very little money, then a glittering rainbow after all the stormy years: he sold a short story to *American Magazine* entitled *Cross Your Heart* for $850. This was the first substantial check ever received for his writings and shortly thereafter he submitted his first factual magazine piece to *Cavalier*, an article about so-called suppressed inventions. The piece was accepted. The editor wanted more and John Toland discovered that magazines of the day were much hungrier for interesting pieces of a factual nature than they were for fiction and he began to move toward the career that would make him famous. From that point, in response to the better magazine market for nonfiction, he dropped all effort to write fiction, novels or plays, and wrote factual magazine pieces that were marketed for him by Roger Terrell, an agent who had been editor of the old *Argosy* magazine, a sympathetic, knowledgeable pro in the fields of editing and publishing.

"I learned to use and adapt the published writings of others," Toland says. "I wrote my short magazine pieces from newspaper accounts, magazine pieces, books, and other available in-print sources in the public library as have countless reporters."

Then came the event that marked the change in his career from one of significant lack of success to significant success as an author. Roger Terrell suggested John Toland as the writer for a book about dirigibles, such a book being desired by an editor at Henry Holt & Co., book publishers.

"I did an outline from materials and information I could scrounge from my accustomed sources at the New York Public Library," Toland related. "Apparently Henry Holt was impressed because I got the assignment and a guarantee of an unbelievable, princely sum of $6,500."

In no way could a complete book on so large a subject be written exclusively from previously published material. So, John Toland was forced to go to what are called "original sources." In this case, the U.S. Government Headquarters For Lighter Than Air Craft at Lakehurst, N.J.

There and then it was that John Toland made the discovery that enabled him to eventually write a succession of best-selling books. He says of this career-turning discovery, "It was when I found myself talking to a real, live expert, a basic source, a participant in the story I was writing, that I realized I was getting the real story, facts and color that were much more vital, authentic, important and arrestingly interesting than I had been able to gather and write about from only earlier published sources."

Of course, author Toland does not ignore all published sources.

Records, reports, and written accounts are read and drawn upon, but the important ingredient of in-the-field, basic, primary, exclusive information lifts the resultant writing to superior worth.

His first book thus written from original sources was published in 1957. It was *Ships in the Sky*, the detailed authoritative story of lighter-than-air craft, dirigibles.

Each of the books that came after were written in such a fashion, from original sources. For *Adolf Hitler* he interviewed more than one hundred and fifty people who knew Hitler personally, and were directly involved in his private or public life. So much material was mined for this book that Toland and his editor trimmed more than one thousand pages from the final manuscript.

John Toland's interview technique is to drain every bit of information on the subject he is pursuing from repeated interviews with the person being interviewed. When finished with this person, John secures from him the names of other persons with additional information on the subject at hand, then talks to these persons, no matter what part of the world they are in. The interviews are recorded on magnetic tape and the tapes are stored in the Congressional Library for reference.

Author Toland is not famed as a literary stylist, but he is an exceptionally able digger of facts and interviewer. His skill is unexcelled in persuading persons to talk without inhibitions into his tape recorder. He has an instinct and personal curiosity that guides him to ask the right questions, and an unflagging diligence in seeking out the right people to interview. He has great courage in asking direct questions, the answers to which may be embarrassing to the person being questioned.

He admits to having a built-in alarm bell which usually rings a warning when someone gives him a false answer. To guard against misinformation he substantiates all statements of fact given him, or found in print, from more than one source.

Earlier, I mentioned there might be a pattern for you to follow in John Toland's record of turning adversity into success. Perhaps, like him, you have been unsuccessful at writing fiction, although you have worked hard in your effort. Certainly, the record of writing six novels, numerous plays, and many short stories are evidences of his ambition, and you may have similar evidence of your own industry. No doubt the early writing he did sharpened his tools as you may have sharpened yours.

It would seem in spite of John Toland's ambition to write fiction, it was not to be. Eventually he has found the satisfaction and

170

rewards he sought for so many years in writing factual books. Possibly you could also.

Not to take anything away from Mr. Toland's enormous, deserved success as an author, it is my observation there are many newspaper and magazine writers who might write books with even more narrative skill and more entertainingly than does he.

It is my conviction there are many able persons who could write successful books if they were to pick a subject in which the reading public is interested; mine their facts from original sources, as does Mr. Toland; then, bring their perseverance and writing skills to the task.

SHOULD YOU WRITE A NOVEL OR A NONFICTION BOOK?

You have now arrived at YOUR MOMENT OF TRUTH. It is decision time.

Will you write a nonfiction book or a novel?

Or are you going to procrastinate? Continue to toss off a non-chalant, boastful, really-don't-mean-it, "Someday I'm going to write a book."

Those of you who are really capable have by now reached a decision to write a book.

Say it and do it! Tell yourself privately and confidently, "I'm going to write a book, NOW!"

You know there is no magic or mystery involved in doing it, no cut-and-dried pattern for writing a book. You must do the job your own way, with what knowledge, ability, ambition, and dedication are yours.

You have been helped on your way to becoming a writer by an inside view of publishing that should dispel any destructive, precon-ceived notion you may have had that publishing is an exotic never-never world, apart and above the everyday commercial world. You know now such is not the case. Publishing is a commercial business, ready to accept the application and contributions of able, ambitious men and women, as are the professions of law, parenthood, medi-cine, homemaking, teaching, baseball, or you-name-it.

Now for some down-to-earth, practical advice that, hopefully, will pull your trigger, get your wheels rolling, and your words on paper.

172

Also, a bit later, I'm going to give you a surprise bonus, a gift of "Archimedes' Secret." This alone may start you writing and keep you writing.

First, in the advice line, you must have a regular place in which to write, one where you will not be disturbed or distracted.

This place of yours can be an upended box in the basement next to the furnace or, if you are fortunate, a room of your own with typewriter, dictionary, no telephone, and a lock on the door. If you are a housewife, a corner in the living room, kitchen, or dining room may be where you can sneak an hour for writing when the kids are in school or in bed.

And don't pity yourself if the only place you can find to write is on the dining room table. Mario Puzo wrote *The Godfather* and his first two novels on his dining room table. Indeed, when he was hired by Paramount to do the screen play of his novel, and brought to California for the job, so productive had been that dining room table, he persuaded Paramount that the only place he could write was in his dining room on that table, so back he went to Long Island to finish the treatment.

However, when fame and fortune embraced Mario, he built a studio annex to his Long Island home and said good-by to his dining room for everything but eating. In this studio he put every writing convenience, an executive type desk, air conditioner, refrigerator, venetian blinds, bookcases, a private phone. Then he closed his studio door against all the large family and other household noises he had endured for so long and started to write a novel to follow *The Godfather*.

You guessed it. The new writing conditions didn't suit him, and after a period of unsatisfactory progress he went back to his dining room table, the typewriter uncomfortably almost as high as his chin, and the novel started to flow. He's back in his studio now, but the transition has not been easy. His new book has been more than four years in the writing.

No matter what, find yourself a place to write and use it regularly every day.

How to find time to write?

That's up to you. It is unlikely you will emulate Norah Lofts and work a long writing day, seven days a week. It is unlikely you will spend your nights writing, your days sleeping, as does Taylor Caldwell. It is more likely you will dedicate one hour, two hours, or maybe three each day.

If your ambition is real you will find the time as have many others, including Sol Stein, president of the large, flourishing book publishing house, Stein and Day. Sol gets out of bed each morning before seven, prepares his own breakfast, and writes at a typewriter on his current novel-in-work until nine o'clock. Then Sol takes off for his publishing office where he concentrates a full working day on publishing the books of other authors. Sol has written six novels on this regime, to the wonderment of his associates, each published by a publishing house other than his own, and is now writing his seventh. Earlier in his career as a moonlighting author, he used to arise at 4:00 A.M. and work until 8. Now he says the writing comes easier the more he writes and he can get as much written in two hours or so as he used to produce in four hours. It is his belief that the more experienced you become in writing the more your writing can lead you. At least he finds he can write a novel without the extensive preplanning and outlining he found necessary when he began writing. For Sol the period just before he goes to sleep is the most valuable and productive period for planning ahead as to where his story will go the next morning when he sits down to write again. Sol's best known novels are *The Magician*, *Living Room*, and *The Childkeeper*.

Sol writes every day for a minimum period, keeping everlastingly at the novel he is working on, even though what he produces may have to be thrown away.

"Sometimes I write what I know to be useless, even drivel," he says, "just so I will keep writing. Sooner or later I know I will be back on the track and move forward on my story if I keep pounding those keys until my regular period for writing is over."

Perhaps had many others kept to this regime, they would have a published novel to their credit instead of an unfinished manuscript.

Another author who refuses to let circumstances prevent him from his ambition to write a novel is Ed Roth, president of the large importing firm, W. A. Taylor & Co. Ed's business responsibilities keep him almost constantly in motion, flying back and forth to England, Scotland, and the principal cities of this continent. When he decided to write a novel, Ed Roth bought several dozen ruled composition books. Instead of reading books or napping in an airplane seat, Ed wrote and wrote and wrote while flying. Instead of watching TV in his hotel room or tasting the nightlife in world capitals, as well he might considering the bulk of his wallet, Ed sat down at the desk in his hotel room night after night and wrote some more in his composition books, all in longhand. Fortunately, Ed has a secretary and a wife who types, and thus was able to mail his handwritten chapters back to his home and office in Miami, Florida, for typing.

A word about handwritten manuscripts. Publishers will not read them or consider them for publication. It is hoped you know how to type, but if you must do your writing in longhand, some provision must be made to produce a typewritten manuscript from your handwritten efforts, a manuscript with your name and address on the first page, upper right-hand corner, and your name on every sequentially numbered page that follows. Be sure to keep at least one accurate carbon copy of your typewritten manuscript in case the original is lost.

How do you start a novel?

That seems to be the single question aspiring novelists ask more often than any other.

The answer: start writing.

Sit down at the typewriter and put words on paper. If the words do not please you, start again, and again, and again, until the words do please you.

Finally you will have developed a momentum, overcome your static inertia, created a forward-moving inertia of your own, and you will be telling a story. Then you are on your way toward constructing a novel. To actually get the project underway, "on the rails and running" so to speak, may take hours, days, or weeks, but keep at it!

The first paragraph of a novel has the utter necessity of interesting and, hopefully, hooking the reader.

An example of first-paragraph "overkill," but one that gets across the idea of attracting the reader might be:

> Young, handsome, obviously virile Roy Winsor brought from his shower by the unexpected ringing of his doorbell, wrapped a scanty towel around his still-dripping midsection and threw wide the door of his bachelor apartment.
>
> There in the hall stood the most stunningly beautiful girl he had ever seen, anywhere, anytime, a smile of amused invitation on her pouted lips, and not a stitch of clothing on any curve or graceful part of her alluring body. Not a single, obscuring stitch. Not one.

Inspect the first paragraph of any successful novel, and you will observe that the author has turned salesman as concerns that first paragraph.

Why? Because experience has shown that bookstore shoppers almost always read the first paragraph of a novel or book to which they have been attracted.

Usually the shopper first inspects the copy on the back cover or inside cover flap. If still interested by what he has read, or whatever attracted him to the book in the first place, the reader turns to and reads the first paragraph of the book.

In so doing he evidences the fact that he wants to be interested, beguiled, and convinced. He is looking for an excuse to buy, a reason to buy, and if that first paragraph entices and hooks the shopper a sale is made.

Some authors solicit the reader's attention in that all-important first paragraph with great subtlety and success. Others shoot off fireworks and fire cannons, but each uses his own brand of skill to grab that reader's attention and interest and make that sale.

Perhaps the most common fault beginners make in starting a novel is to back into their story. Many a discerning editor has pushed his way through two, three, four, or ten first pages of a manuscript, then sat up as though goosed by an electric prod. "Here's where the novel starts," exclaims the editor happily, "right here on page eight," and proceeds to cross out everything the author has written up to that point.

Certainly the sooner you can get into your story and interest your reader, the better.

For those of you who ache to write a novel there is something in you that wants out.

Yours is the classic fabled situation of the genie in the bottle, and you are the bottle.

No magic word or rubbing of a bottle or your forehead will release this genie. You are pregnant with an obsession and your only release lies in abortion or birth. Your salvation is to put words on paper. Tell your story. Keep everlastingly at it, writing and rewriting until you are satisfied to have published what you have written.

Do not be surprised that what you wrote yesterday may not be accepted by you today. Be happy that tomorrow you may want to do over and make better what you have written today.

To write and rewrite are, in themselves, real and meaningful progress, and by so doing you are learning and growing from your own efforts.

Keep at the writing and rewriting of your novel until you have some pages you believe are in final, satisfying form. Then push on, over and past all obstacles, until you have a complete, finished, satisfying draft of the novel, one you believe ready for publication, ready to be read and enjoyed by others.

How does one ambitious to write a nonfiction book go about it?

There is one simple, helpful suggestion for a writer of nonfiction that does not apply equally to the writing of a novel.

It is this: Almost all nonfiction books are written "me-to-you." The author is speaking directly to his readers as though standing before them.

With this in mind a nonfiction book can be written as a long, very personal letter to a friend you value and respect.

Thus your nonfiction book will have the responsibility of being warmly informative, interestingly and personally presented for the entertainment and interest of your "friend." In this case your "friend" is a friendly audience, one interested in whatever is the subject of your nonfiction book. Friendly and receptive or the audience would not have picked up your book.

A word of caution. Do not put any misinformation in this "long letter to a friend." A nonfiction book must be as factual as you can write it. You cannot be less than honest, as indeed you would not be in a letter to a friend.

If you have any doubt concerning a single statement of fact in your book, research it and be prepared to prove the truth of your statement.

While most nonfiction books can be written as a "letter to a friend," such is not the case with a novel. It takes a very special type of fiction story to be told in letter form. Mickey Spillane has written all of his famous Mike Hammer novels in the first person, and the classic Sherlock Holmes novels are recited thus by the ubiquitous Doctor Watson. On the whole, beware of the first person novel, unless there is a valid literary or logical reason for telling your story in that form. It is generally believed more difficult to write a successful novel in the first person and many editors confess to a prejudice against them.

Most of the methods or manners of telling a fictional story hold true for the writer of nonfiction. Usually the nonfiction writer has a wider choice of subjects or themes to write about at any given moment. Some novelists, however, are fortunate in having ideas for a number of novels in their minds as they work on one book, and a few, like the late Erle Stanley Gardner, write as many as three novels simultaneously. These are exceptions. Most writers of novels are happy to have one story to which they can apply themselves at that point in time. A professional writer of nonfiction may have several subjects waiting his investigation, research, and writing, and he may even work on books of different subjects at the same time as events unfold or research materials become available. No doubt an author's first nonfiction book is best written about a subject with which he is very familiar, rather than a theme he must research from scratch.

In that category of familiar subjects may be textbooks written by teachers concerning their very familiar specialty. I have no knowledge of, or experience in, the textbook field, so if it is your desire to write a textbook I suggest you corner one of the numerous publisher's representatives, whose job is to sell textbooks to schools and find textbook authors. Ask him how to go about it. Or, better yet, ask a text-writing colleague for information.

Factual books far outnumber fictional books in number of titles published. The category outsells fiction, too, although all-time best-selling titles are predominately fiction books.

A definition of a best-selling nonfiction book is simply: "An easy-to-read, interest-grabbing recital about anything real or true that readers enjoy and feel compelled to tell others about."

If you have all of that in one book you have a potential bestseller. If you have some or most of it you have a successful book.

Timeliness and public interest in the subject has a lot to do with the success of a factual book, as is repeatedly proven by the many successful sports figure biographies, confessions, and as-told-to autobiographies of these sports heroes and other persons in the public eye. Well-publicized events, such as the Watergate scandals, give birth to many books by both participants and observers. Of course, not every would-be writer has access to firsthand involvement in a Watergate or opportunity to be Boswell to a sports hero.

Lacking these opportunities, there is a very good chance you can write a readable, publishable book on any subject you can talk interestingly and authoritatively about with the narrative skill necessary to hold an audience's attention.

Literally, a nonfiction book can be written about any conceivable topic. To give you an idea of how varied such books can be, here are a few subjects of recently published successful nonfiction books: airplane disaster, experiences of a veterinarian, experiences of a doctor, experiences of a lawyer, experiences of a teacher, transcendental meditation, houseplants, a pet quail, a dog, a cat, LSD, dreams, gifted child, arthritis, pocket watches, the occult, business methods, orgasm, diet, sex, how to study, golf, chess, bridge, prostitutes, terrariums, guns, poker, gin rummy, butterflies, etc.

The examples of successful book subjects listed above are not intended as a list from which you might select topics to write a book about, but to demonstrate that the ideas for nonfiction books are without limit.

It is the subject matter and the facts in the nonfiction book that are basically responsible for the reader's interest in any factual book, accepting, of course, that the nonfiction book must be written skillfully and in an intriguing, entertaining manner. Who wrote the nonfiction best-seller usually does not matter to the purchaser. Such a book is more likely to be bought for what is in it than as a response to the name of the author, as is sometimes the case with a novel.

So your chances for publication are probably better if you author a nonfiction book, rather than a novel.

Still, be you a would-be factual writer or novelist, take heart in the fact that there is only one commodity in the book publishing business in short supply. It's not paper, presses, or editors—it's authors!

Once your novel or book is finished, or partially finished, beware of soliciting advice, criticism, or opinion concerning the manuscript from a friend, a local teacher, someone who "reads a lot," or anyone except a professional editor, hopefully an editor employed by a publisher who has shown an interest in publishing your book.

That editor has a right to suggest changes in your work because of his knowledge and experience and because it is his company that is willing to gamble on publishing your writing.

Even then, if the editor makes suggestions for changes, you should not make the changes unless you can, after reflective thought, agree that such changes will better the book or, at the very least, make it no less good in your judgment.

A professional editor can come up often with a suggestion for change in a manuscript that rings a happy response in the writer. "Why didn't I think of that?" he asks himself as he bends happily to making changes he realizes will improve his brain-child.

Do not, however, trust your Aunt Hattie, the local high school English teacher, your wife, or your husband to make trustworthy or meaningful criticisms of your manuscript. To solicit or receive such unprofessional advice may be as deadly dangerous as treating yourself for the cure of pneumonia with a medical prescription concocted by your friendly garage mechanic.

To solicit, receive, or be exposed to unprofessional advice about what you have written may head you in wrong directions and up unfamiliar one-way roads from which you will never return, if you attempt to write as someone else thinks you should. Or if the outside opinions of your writing are praise and flattery, your own critical apparatus may be so thrown out of balance you will be forever incapable of evaluating your own work objectively, conned by some well-meaning praise bestower into the horrifying belief that to erase a word of your prose is comparable to hacking a leg off the Venus de Milo.

Particularly can such amateur criticisms be damaging when you are in the beginning stages of cultivating yourself as a creator, someone whose manner of writing, thoughts, and expressions must reflect your own very personal stamp of originality. In short, an author.

So once you have decided to write a book—novel or nonfiction—do so with the knowledge that writing is necessarily a lonely, but happily so, business.

A meaningful analogy can be drawn between you writing a book by yourself and a carpenter building a house single-handedly. Each of you uses simple tools to accomplish your respective jobs. You have the words, narrative skills, and desire to build your structure. The carpenter has nails, hammer, saw, plane, and will to erect his structure. How each of you expresses individual skills and taste in your individual endeavors will decide how attractive and appealing to others is the house or book.

But in the building of your structure you, the author, have a dramatic advantage. You can rip out and redo any part of your book at any time during the construction, and thus refine, reshape, and improve your original structure as you progress; and by so doing, learn your craft as a writer "on-the-job" as it were.

Given the author's privilege of shaping, changing, and improving, a diligent writer sometimes comes up with a completely stunning accomplishment with his first, finally completed, book.

Writing can never be an easy job.

That is a fact of authorship I hope you have learned from this book.

Another is that no publisher wants to reject a book.

Still another is that as a writer you will have your good days, your dark days, your triumphs, and your failures.

When you need encouragement, it is my hope you will find new strength and determination by rereading the parts of this book which relate to the experiences of authors who persisted and persevered.

And if that doesn't do it, herewith Archimedes' Secret, as promised a few pages back.

"What is Archimedes' Secret?" you ask.

"Archimedes discovered the principle of the lever—discovered the lever—so to speak," I remind you. "But that is not the secret I have just for you. . . ."

"Just for me?"

"For you alone. But first another reminder. Archimedes is quoted as having said, 'Give me a lever long enough, a place to stand, and I will move the world,' right?"

"Yes," you agree. "He is supposed to have said something like that."

"Now listen carefully. If you really want to write a book, *really* want to write a book, you have qualified to use the secret and here it is: As a writer you have a 'long, strong lever,' your ability. Your 'place to stand' is your personal perspective, a vantage point outside the world of anyone else and uniquely your own. Stand there, apply the force of your ambition to the lever of your ability and you will move the world, or at least that part of the world that reads your book.

"Push hard. Keep pushing."